INSPIRING BEAUTY

INSPIRING

50 Years of

EDITED BY Joy L. Bivins and Rosemary K. Adams

BEAUTY

Ebony Fashion Fair

CHICAGO HISTORY MUSEUM

INSPIRING BEAUTY | 50 YEARS OF EBONY FASHION FAIR

The exhibition *Inspiring Beauty: 50 Years of Ebony Fashion Fair* was on display in the Bessie Green-Field Warshawsky Gallery, The Mazza Foundation Gallery, and the Skyline Gallery of the Pritzker Foundation Special Exhibitions Wing at the Chicago History Museum from March 16, 2013 through May 11, 2014.

Published in the United States of America by the Chicago Historical Society.

Copyright © 2013 by the Chicago Historical Society. All rights reserved.
No part of this publication may be reproduced in any manner whatsoever without the written permission of the Chicago Historical Society.

Chicago History Museum
1601 N. Clark Street
Chicago, Illinois 60614
www.chicagohistory.org

ISBN: 978-0-913820-37-7

Project Editor: Rosemary K. Adams
Photography: John Alderson
Design and production: Glue + Paper Workshop LLC, Chicago
   www.glueandpaper.com
Color separations: Embassy Graphics, Winnipeg, Manitoba, Canada
Printing: Friesens Corporation, Altona, Manitoba, Canada

Second printing produced by International Arts & Artists
9 Hillyer Court NW, Washington, DC 20008
www.artsandartists.org

Printed in the USA through Four Colour Print Group, Louisville, Kentucky.

Photography credits:

Pages 2–3, 12, 14–22, 26, 29, 32, 42, 43 (right), 46 (left), 51, 59, 68, 80, 89, 91, 94, 102, 103, 107–109, 122, 125, 127–129, 136: courtesy of Johnson Publishing Corporation LLC.

Pages 9–10, 38, 41, 43 (left), 44, 45, 46 (right), 47, 52–58, 60, 61, 63–67, 69–77, 79, 81, 82–88, 90, 93, 95–99, 101, 104, 105, 110, 111, 113–121, 123, 126, 130–135: photography by John Alderson, © Chicago Historical Society.

Page 27: © Chicago Historical Society.

CONTENTS

Exhibition Sponsors 6

Foreword 11

Preface/Acknowledgments 12

STYLE AND SUBSTANCE: *Ebony's* Fashion Fair 14
    Joy L. Bivins

RESPECT AND PLEASURE: The Meaning of Style in African American Life 28
    Maxine Leeds Craig

THE POWER OF FASHION: Ebony Fashion Fair 38
    Virginia Heaven

SELECTIONS FROM THE EXHIBITION 53

EXHIBITION SPONSORS

Inspiring Beauty: 50 Years of Ebony Fashion Fair was developed by the Chicago History Museum in cooperation with Johnson Publishing Company, LLC.

Presented by the Costume Council of the Chicago History Museum

Chicago Presenting Partner

HOST COMMITTEE

Exelon
J.B. and M.K. Pritzker Family Foundation
Col. (IL) J. N. Pritzker, IL ARNG (Retired)
Tawani Foundation
The Joyce Foundation
Fifth Third Bank
Cari and Michael J. Sacks
Neiman Marcus

ELITE

CIRCA

PRESIDENT'S CIRCLE

Constance and David Coolidge
Bon and Holly French
    and Adams Street Partners
David D. Hiller
Cindy and Andrew H. Kalnow
Saks Fifth Avenue
Liz Stiffel

BENEFACTOR

Kate Boege
Choose Chicago
Catherine and Reed Eberle
Columbia College Chicago
Vicki and Bill Hood
Nena Ivon
Juanita Vanoy Jordan
Dr. Katie Klehr
Mesirow Financial
Erica C. Meyer
Mr. and Mrs. Lucius Reese
Patrick G. and Shirley W. Ryan Foundation
Mr. and Mrs. Greg Shearson
The Abra Wilkin Fund

PATRON

James L. Alexander and Curtis D. Drayer
Ariel Investments
Christopher and Margaret Block
Sherrill and John Bodine
Mr. and Mrs. Richard Canada
Mr. and Mrs. Michael Cherry
Marcia Cohn
Mr. and Mrs. Joseph Spencer Cotten
Mr. and Mrs. Chris Dunagan
B. Michael and Mark-Anthony Edwards
Richard and Melissa Gamble
Mr. and Mrs. William M. Goodyear, Jr.
Mr. and Mrs. Michael Golden
Mirja & Ted Haffner Family Fund
Margaret J. Harris
Michael R. Hawley
Mr. Thomas W. Hawley and Mr. Tom Mantel
Marci and Ronald Holzer
Mr. and Mrs. Tobin E. Hopkins

Gregory Hyder
Mr. and Mrs. Gary T. Johnson
Judy and Dave Lockhart
Stuart and George Mesires
neapolitan collection
Phyllis Rabineau
Anthony F. Rossi
Elizabeth Ryan
Laura Barnett Sawchyn
April T. Schink
Kristin Smith
Diane G. Sprenger
Dr. and Mrs. Alexander Stemer
Ruth Thuston
Mindy and Andrew Turitz
Richard and Noren Ungaretti
Mr. and Mrs. Daniel Waters
Mr. and Mrs. Robert Zentner
Bill Zwecker and Tom Gorman

TOUR SCHEDULE

Inspiring Beauty: 50 Years of Ebony Fashion Fair exhibition tour was organized by International Arts & Artists (IA&A), Washington, DC. The tour, from October 2014 to December 2017, featured 41 of the 67 garments in the Chicago History Museum's presentation of the exhibition. IA&A is a non-profit organization dedicated to increasing cross-cultural understanding and exposure to the arts internationally through exhibitions, programs, and services artists, arts institutions, and the public.

Museum of Design Atlanta, GA
October 18, 2014–January 4, 2015

Milwaukee Art Museum, WI
February 5–May 3, 2015

Minnesota History Center, St. Paul, MN
May 22–August 16, 2015

Charles H. Wright Museum of
African American History, Detroit, MI
September 18, 2015–January 3, 2016

Memorial Art Gallery
of the University of Rochester, NY
January 30–April 24, 2016

Bellevue Arts Museum, WA
May 20–August 14, 2016

The George Washington University Museum
and The Textile Museum, Washington, DC
Winter–Summer 2017

For a complete tour schedule please visit:
www.artsandartists.org

FOREWORD

MY MOTHER, EUNICE W. JOHNSON, was the dynamic, elegant, and uncompromising architect behind the Ebony Fashion Fair show. As she merged her passion for fashion with her commitment to local communities, she earned her place among the fashion-elite by creating her own rules.

Through travels to the world's fashion capitals, she discovered the most show stopping designs. The Ebony Fashion Fair show was created to be far more than a simple display of glamorous pieces of art; it was created to reflect the highest standards of Johnson Publishing Company and celebrate the best that fashion had to offer. She transcended color lines through sheer determination, proving she was truly a woman ahead of her time.

I am grateful for the foundation my mother laid and proud of the legacy she built. With principal, purpose and her impeccable taste, the world of fashion was revolutionized and the way Black women see themselves was changed forever.

Linda Johnson Rice
Johnson Publishing Company

PREFACE/ACKNOWLEDGMENTS

BETWEEN 1940 AND 1960, the first two decades of the Second Great Migration, Chicago's African American population grew from 278,000 to 813,000. This enormous influx overwhelmed the city; Chicago's South Side black neighborhoods were literally bursting their seams, and tensions escalated with white residents who saw this black surge as a threat to their own communities. Chicago was a divided city, and African Americans faced a legion of difficult challenges: employment discrimination, overcrowded and dilapidated housing, poor schools, growing crime, and intense outbursts of racial violence directed against them. Despite these dispiriting conditions, Chicago was spotlighted as the capital of black America. Home to Congressman William L. Dawson, the nation's most powerful black politician, Joe Louis, America's beloved boxing champion, and the electric blues, personified in the music of Muddy Waters, Chicago was also the center for black business entrepreneurs.

Within this dynamic crucible of black enterprise and urban change, John H. Johnson launched *Ebony* magazine in 1945. It was an instant success, and its circulation exploded. Johnson drew on a powerful legacy of black journalism and entrepreneurship that grew in Chicago in the first half of the twentieth century. While the *Chicago Defender* had become the most widely read and most important black metropolitan newspaper in America through its unwavering stand on civil rights, *Ebony* spoke to African Americans as consumers. As publisher, Johnson did not shy away from civil rights issues and stories about racial discrimination, but he recognized African Americans untapped potential as a market for mainstream American services and products and filled his magazine with advertisements for luxury goods and aspirational images of success. Economic success, Johnson argued, spawned political power and social advancement. Shaping black consumer behavior was a key editorial strategy of the magazine's editors, and articles about how to appreciate art and music or how to dress and entertain provided friendly advice to help readers buy wisely and thus establish and maintain their status as middle-class Americans. *Ebony* was thus more than a monthly publication about African Americans; it was a lifestyle brand.

Expanding Fashion Fair from a feature in the magazine to a charity event was a shrewd business decision that greatly enhanced the *Ebony* brand, and the runway became another powerful venue for extolling *Ebony*'s success-based vision of African-Americans. But strengthening the brand was not the only motive behind launching the fair. The upper echelons of fashion design—Parisian- and Italian-based based haute couture—was off limits to African American women, but Eunice Johnson was determined to break down the walls that excluded blacks from participating as designers, model, and as consumers. And she succeeded through a determined effort and a bankroll. Ebony Fashion Fair exceeded John and Eunice Johnson's expectations for strengthening the *Ebony* brand and as a fundraising event for charity. But it was also a catalyst for social change and cultural transformation that nobody could have imagined. It made manifest the civil rights struggle for women on a visceral and emotional level; it was a community celebration of black pride and style that resonated in high school gymnasiums and church basements throughout America; it jumpstarted and spurred the evolution of black beauty and black fashion; and it launched the careers of countless African

American models, makeup artists, hairdressers, and fashion designers—beauty and fashion professionals who continue to inspire and influence new generations through their legacies or their latest creations.

Inspiring Beauty: 50 Years of Ebony Fashion Fair tells the remarkable story of an extraordinary fashion show. Drawing on Johnson Publishing Company's extensive holdings of Fashion Fair garments, *Inspiring Beauty* showcases more than sixty ensembles, interpreting them through the lenses of color, innovation, and power, and chronicling the half-century the show flourished and its ongoing impact in America.

This exhibition and catalogue would never have come to fruition without the initial inspiration and steadfast support from Linda Johnson Rice and Gary T. Johnson. The unique partnership they fostered between Johnson Publishing Company and the Chicago History Museum and their shared vision for an exhibition on the history of the Ebony Fashion Fair was the catalyst for this project and an ongoing source of encouragement during its development. Nena Ivon, chair of the Costume Council of the Chicago History Museum enthusiastically endorsed *Inspiring Beauty* from the very beginning and spearheaded the Costume Council's extraordinary support. She, too, has been an incredible partner throughout this enterprise. I also want to especially acknowledge the extremely generous support of the many individuals who adopted one of the garments in the exhibition through our Sponsor of Style program.

"It takes a staff to conceive, develop, and build an exhibition" is the museum equivalent of the African proverb, "It takes a village to raise a child," and *Inspiring Beauty* is a perfect example of the level of dedication and the intense nature of the work that characterize these endeavors. Timothy A. Long, former curator of costumes, forged the initial contact with Johnson Publishing Company to explore the idea of an exhibition on the history of Ebony Fashion Fair. Joy Bivins, curator at the Chicago History Museum, built on preliminary research to create the interpretive framework that presents these examples of extraordinary fashion design within the historical context of five decades of the Fashion Fair. Her enthusiasm, storytelling skills, and her hard work are evident in every aspect of the exhibition and in this publication. Her efforts to enrich the Fashion Fair story and to make it more accessible to broader and more diverse audiences is especially gratifying. Virginia Heaven, assistant professor in fashion studies at Columbia College, served as consulting curator for the exhibition; her impeccable knowledge of fashion history and her sense of style animate the exhibition in powerful ways. Ms. Bivins and Ms. Heaven formed an awesome pairing, and I am grateful for their team effort.

The exhibition, publication, and public and youth programs would not have been possible without the hard work and dedication of the entire staff of the Chicago History Museum. Phyllis Rabineau brought overall leadership to all aspects of the project, and I am grateful for her perseverance and guiding hand. Special thanks to Rosemary Adams, Randy Adamsick, John Alderson, Alexander Aubrey, Marne Bariso, Julie Benner, Tamara Biggs, Dean Brobst, Ilana Bruton, Nancy Buenger, Mimi de Castro, Emma Denny, Ginny Fitzgerald, Elizabeth Garibay, Nicholas Glenn, Calvin Gray, Jessica Harvey, Rob Jeffries, Julie Katz, Fredi Leaf, Kathleen Ludwig, Holly Lundberg, Lynn McRainey, Heidi Moisan, Emily Nordstrom, Cheryl Obermeyer, Dan Oliver, Sam Plourd, Mark Ramirez, John Russick, Emma Sawyer, William Stafford, Carol Turchan, and Sandra Yatsko.

I want to extend special thanks to the staff at Johnson Publishing Company for their spirit of collaboration, for generously providing access to the company's historical materials, and for their willingness to share their knowledge of and enthusiasm for Ebony Fashion Fair. In particular, we are grateful to Kenneth Marlon Owen, Crystal Howard, and Vickie Wilson.

Russell Lewis
Executive Vice President and Chief Historian
Chicago History Museum

Joy L. Bivins

STYLE AND SUBSTAN

For five decades, Chicago-based Johnson Publishing Company's traveling fashion show, Ebony Fashion Fair, brought the best in international and American fashion to majority black and female audiences across the United States in a spectacle of performance and entertainment. During the two-hour show, African American women saw reflections of themselves in garments that few people from any racial demographic see up close and personal. More than a simple display of exquisite ensembles, Ebony Fashion Fair also reflected the goals and objectives of Johnson Publishing Company to visually showcase and celebrate the best in black life. This essay examines the history and significance of the traveling fashion show as a reflection of that mission, the *Ebony* brand, and the ways in which both the fashion show and Johnson Publishing projected new images of blackness. It also explores the groundbreaking work of Eunice Walker Johnson, Ebony Fashion Fair's longtime producer and director. Her work to shape the traveling show, created a unique performance of fashion and style. Through the show, she shared her access to the world of high fashion to *Ebony*'s readers and helped open doors for African Americans within that often-closed world.

By the time famed model Iman graced the cover of the 1983 Ebony Fashion Fair program in a striking gown by Pierre Cardin, *Ebony* readers were used

Ebony's *Fashion Fair*

to such unabashed displays of black female beauty. Likewise, Ebony Fashion Fair attendees had come to expect the high level of fashion featured on the program cover in the show. Indeed, that year's theme, "Fashion Extravaganza," summed up what the traveling show had become since its debut in 1958. Johnson Publishing Company had set the bar high in terms of the designers featured in *Ebony* and in the two-hour show. But from the start, Ebony Fashion Fair was about more than just beautiful clothes. To be sure, the fashion was fabulous but mission and brand as well as charity were critical.

The story of *Ebony*'s traveling show begins simply enough.[1] In 1956, Jessie Dent, wife of Dillard University's president, approached John H. Johnson about supplying models for a charity fundraiser for Flint-Goodridge Hospital located on the school's New Orleans campus. Fashion show fundraisers were not new, and they were especially popular throughout the South, but Johnson was reluctant to share the models he used in his company's magazines. He offered instead to supply the clothing, and Dent agreed. Johnson's offer, however, was accompanied by a very critical caveat: each ticket would include a subscription to either *Jet* or *Ebony* magazine. The show was successful, and in 1958 Johnson Publishing Company launched a traveling fashion show. Aspects of the original formula were repeated for five decades as the Ebony Fashion Fair grew into what the publishing giant dubbed the "world's largest traveling fashion show."[2]

From 1958 through 2009, the show's most recent season, the Ebony Fashion Fair brought some of the world's most exclusive fashion to hundreds of thousands of eager attendees across the United States, Canada, and the Caribbean. During its first season, the show traveled to thirty cities, and at its height, Fashion Fair models performed in 187 venues to crowds that could exceed five thousand. Along the way, the traveling show raised money for African American charities and served as a platform for reinforcing the Johnson Publishing Company's mission and brand identity. Like Johnson publications, the Fashion Fair projected the most positive images of African Americans and, consequently, black life to majority African American audiences.

Ebony Fashion Fair was an extravagant performance, whether it took place in a grand ballroom or a high school auditorium.[3] The show's format was established in those early days, and even the earliest show included one-hundred ensembles. In general, there were two acts with scenes featuring daywear, swimwear, and evening wear punctuated by a musical intermission. Always an event that exuded elegance and glamour, the Ebony Fashion Fair early on established itself as a significant social event for African Americans, especially those who identified as middle- and upper-middle-class.

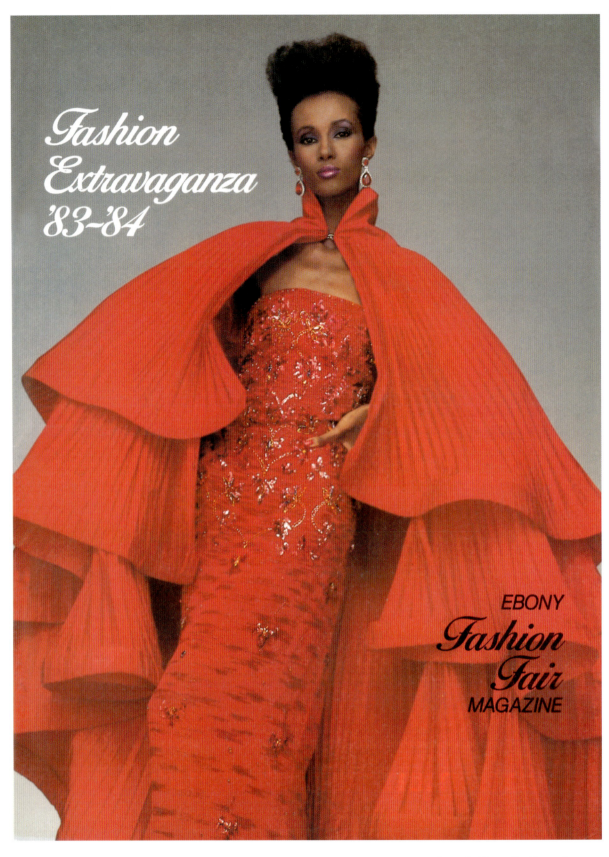

Iman in Pierre Cardin on the 1983–84 program cover.

The society pages of local black newspapers heavily covered the shows, reporting on the prices of ensembles, the abilities of the models, notable attendees, and what they wore.

Part of Ebony Fashion Fair's quick ascendance in African American social circles could certainly be attributed to audiences' familiarity with the family of Johnson publications, *Negro Digest*, *Tan*, *Hue*, *Jet*, and especially *Ebony*. Published for the first time in November 1945, the pictorial magazine had not only gained popularity but prominence within African American households. Taking its cue from the popular pictorial magazines of the era, such as *Life* and *Look*, *Ebony* spoke to an audience hungry for visual representations of itself that highlighted the positive aspects of their lives and showcased possibilities for success. And because *Ebony* filled that void, black communities voraciously consumed it. *Ebony* readers were well aware of the Fashion Fair feature within the magazine—the beautiful garments as well as the beautiful women featured in them. The chance to see the traveling show then, in many ways, was a chance to see the feature in real space and time.

As *Ebony* grew, so did the traveling fashion show. During the 1960s, the show's reputation and reach grew as did the producers' access to international fashion, especially French design. By the 1970s, the Ebony Fashion Fair was an established institution, with a tried and true formula, and in the middle of the decade the show expanded to a two-part season beginning in the fall and ending in the spring. During the next decade, Ebony Fashion Fair continued its growth as the show traveled to more than 180 cities and featured 200 ensembles or exits. Although Ebony Fashion Fair remained an important social event and fundraiser in the 1990s, new challenges arose. Complete ensembles became difficult to purchase, audiences had new avenues for accessing high fashion, and a new generation of attendees yearned to see new visions of themselves. Additionally, and importantly, the cultural landscape had changed, and in some sense, the necessity of projecting positive images of blackness was no longer the radical act it was when the show began. Ironically, Johnson's publications and the Ebony Fashion Fair helped facilitate that change.

Despite these challenging factors, the Ebony Fashion Fair remained one of the most unique experiences of fashion and performance anywhere. Charismatic models continued to inhabit and perform in over-the-top costume, charities still raised money for worthwhile causes, and Johnson Publishing Company continued to use fashion to promote the unlimited possibilities of black life.

JOHNSON PUBLISHING COMPANY: PROJECTING BLACKNESS

When John Johnson introduced his first publication, *Negro Digest*, in November 1942, he did so on a wing and a prayer. Despite his connections to some of Chicago's most prominent African American businessmen, Johnson was unable to obtain a small business loan to get *Negro Digest* off the ground. As the legend goes, he secured a $500 loan from his mother, Gertrude Johnson, who leveraged her highly prized furniture suite. Her son quickly made good on the investment as the publication, with a format similar to the highly popular *Reader's Digest*, became an instant success.[4] Soon, Johnson was looking to expand his business with a new venture, which he accomplished with the introduction of *Ebony* in November 1945.

The impact of *Ebony* on black culture was quick and stunning. Despite the lack of color photography during the magazine's first year, *Ebony* appealed to African American audiences, and the magazine quickly outpaced *Negro Digest*. Johnson clearly understood that black people enjoyed pictorial magazines, such as *Life* and *Look*, as much as other Americans; more important, he was keenly aware of African Americans' desire to see more authentic and positive images of themselves. Thus, from the serial's earliest days, Johnson Publishing employed a formula that focused on African American success, aspiration, and accomplishment. The lives of black celebrities, achievers, and heroes were an essential element of the *Ebony* convention and its success.

As *Ebony* grew in popularity and prominence, Johnson Publishing Company introduced new publications. *Jet*, a weekly newsmagazine launched in November 1951, was among them. *Jet*, like *Ebony* and all other Johnson serials, referenced the color black and was conceived as a pocket-sized, weekly newsmagazine that reported on the happenings of "Negroes" all over

The second year of the Ebony Fashion Fair, 1959

the United States. Not straying far from the formula established in *Ebony* of featuring black celebrities, beauties, and other extraordinary personalities, the weekly's first cover featured Edna Robinson, wife of famed boxer Sugar Ray Robinson. *Jet* was followed by *Hue*, *Tan Confessions*, and *Tan*, each taking a cue from an already popular magazine but featuring African Americans. Johnson knew that his audience would purchase media that privileged their experiences, even if those experiences were exceptional.

According to historian Adam Green, Johnson Publishing Company's serials, starting with *Negro*

A group of women attending an Ebony Fashion Fair, c. 1959

Digest, used a strategy of portraying black life and imagination in a nuanced and complex manner. In other words, the problem of blackness in a racist and racialized society was not privileged as the core of black life. Green argues that *Ebony* sought to answer theorist Alain Locke's call that black people base notions of group identity upon a shared life, rather than a common problem.[5] What was the common problem? Centuries-long experiences with institutionalized and violent racism that excluded African Americans from the promise of the American dream. Johnson Publishing serials appeared as World War II ended and African Americans began demanding and strategizing for greater inclusion in the fabric of American life. This new self-consciousness was, in part, informed by Blacks' experiences as servicemen promoting the mantra of American freedom and democracy abroad despite its denial to black Americans at home. *Negro Digest, Ebony, Jet,* and other Johnson periodicals speak to and even help to define a shift in African Americans' self-consciousness during this crucial period on the eve of the modern Civil Rights Movement. The publications addressed issues of racism and race discrimination, at varying degrees depending on the moment, but the main focus was on African American life, success, achievement, and the possibilities of the good life. Green writes:

> The dream world of successes, romances, and life routines of recognizable black personalities was for readers and staff the signature quality of the magazine. It was *Ebony* that originated the specific concept of black celebrity, a structure central to African-American culture today and evocative of deep shifts in racial notion of selfhood since the 1940s.[6]

Ebony and other titles, in essence, captured and reflected shifts in the ways African Americans envisioned life's possibilities in an age of economic expansion and the growth of consumer culture. The formula of Johnson Publishing Company's flagship periodical was indeed centered on black celebrities, such as Lena Horne (who appeared on the magazine's first color cover in 1946), Nat King Cole, and the ever-popular Joe Louis, but it also included features recognizable in any

Cover of *Ebony*, October 1961

Models work the runway during the show's thirty-eighth season, 1996–97.

lifestyle magazine. *Ebony* writers advised readers on travel destinations, the newest recipes, and the latest in women's fashion. By the mid-1950s, *Ebony* included a regular fashion feature edited by Freda DeKnight, the magazine's home service director, entitled Fashion Fair that showed the latest fashion trends on glamorous black models. These representations stood in sharp contrast with images of blackness present within the dominant culture such as Mammy and Jezebel.[7] Yes, the feature allowed readers to catch up on the latest fashion trends but more important, to see images of black women that reflected glamour and elegance not yet projected within mainstream culture. In addition to the regular Fashion Fair feature, *Ebony* included an annual feature of the nation's best-dressed women. Often the wives of prominent black politicians or businessmen, the elegantly clad women were usually photographed in their equally fine homes further reinforcing not just the possibility of acquiring the finer things in life but showcasing that reality for a select few.

Ultimately, Johnson Publishing Company serials were about reflecting a new kind of black experience. That experience was not necessarily rooted in the pain of the past, although that pain could interrupt the new narrative promoted in the company's magazines, but in the realities of the present and the possibilities of the future.[8] Those possibilities most often meant material accumulation and/or the attainment of social status. After all, this was the Johnson family's reality; they built an empire based on the recognition of an underserved, long neglected, often maligned, and upwardly mobile consumer market. Johnson Publishing addressed that market directly and supplied them with images of themselves that were more nuanced, authentic, and, as Adam Green argues, complex than those available in the dominant media culture.[9] The images and features within the company's magazines provided well-to-do and upwardly mobile blacks a more accurate reflection of who they were and hoped to be and gave economically disenfranchised blacks something for which to aspire. Johnson Publishing's periodicals did so with a core belief that, contrary to centuries-old notions, "Black is and should be a color of high esteem."[10]

EUNICE JOHNSON: FASHIONING A LEGACY

Eunice Walker Johnson and her husband and business partner, John, could hardly have come from more different backgrounds. John Johnson was born in Arkansas City, Arkansas, but spent his formative years on Chicago's South Side, establishing himself as a stellar student with a head for business. Eunice Walker was raised in a prominent, upper-middle-class Selma, Alabama, family. Whereas John's mother, Mrs. Gertrude Johnson, worked as a domestic to support her family, Eunice's mother was an educator and her father was a surgeon. Further, she grew up in a family with deep roots and community ties while John's family, like so many other African American families in the early twentieth century, migrated to Chicago in search of better opportunities. Eunice graduated from Talladega College, an historically black college in her home state of Alabama, where she majored in sociology and minored in art while John briefly attended the University of Chicago before committing to working full-time at Chicago's Supreme Life Insurance Company. Despite such different backgrounds, together they worked to build a media empire that centered on the lives, successes, and aspirations of African Americans.

Eunice and John met in Chicago's famed Bronzeville neighborhood in 1940 and were married in her hometown the following year. A little more than a year later, they were publishing *Negro Digest*. As John Johnson pulled the necessary pieces together to launch the magazine, Mrs. Johnson worked during the day as a social worker and assisted her husband with the new publication in the evening.[11] A trusted advisor in the family business, Eunice named the company's flagship publication, *Ebony*.[12] In the magazine's tenth anniversary issue, she, along with John Johnson and his mother, were listed as the principal owners of Johnson Publishing Company. Additionally, Eunice Johnson was listed as the company's secretary-treasurer beginning in the early 1950s, although it is unclear how involved she was in daily financial operations. According to John Johnson, Mrs. Johnson was not yet working full-time for the company in the 1950s but it is clear that from the beginning, Eunice Johnson was an influential presence and force in building Johnson Publishing Company.[13]

Unlike her husband, Eunice Johnson did not write an autobiography detailing her life story and the road

Eunice Johnson at work, 1970

Undated photograph of a young Eunice Johnson

to fame and fortune. Much of what is known about her early life can be viewed as public record. Her family's social standing and educational attainment so early in the twentieth century make her early life exceptional. Not only were her parents professionals in a time when sharecropping and domestic labor were the norm for black workers but her family also had a history of establishing institutions committed to improving the lives of African Americans. Despite the lack of an official biography, Mrs. Johnson was a prolific writer and her subject was one she knew well—fashion. Indeed, Mrs. Johnson recalls an early interest in fashion and style. Through her work as producer and director of *Ebony*'s Fashion Fair, Mrs. Johnson was able to fully explore that interest while projecting and promoting ideas central to the mission and brand of her publishing company.

In 1963, with the death of Freda DeKnight, Mrs. Johnson took over direction of the Fashion Fair traveling show. By 1965, she was *Ebony*'s fashion director. In both outlets, she revealed a keen understanding of fashion trends and the style expectations of her respective audiences. Mrs. Johnson, who was involved with the traveling show from its inception, built on Mrs. DeKnight's early work and transformed Ebony Fashion Fair into a national institution. In the process, she developed long-standing relationships with some of the world's most influential designers, often purchasing from soon-to-be fashion icons early in their careers. Johnson also created opportunities for black talent, from models to fashion designers. Ultimately, she used the traveling show as a platform to project new ideas about what Black women could wear and who they could be—a project very similar to that of *Ebony* and other Johnson Publishing titles.

Part of Fashion Fair's story includes the struggle that both she and Mrs. DeKnight faced in securing garments for those early shows. According to John Johnson, when he and Mrs. Johnson first went to Europe to purchase clothes, they "had to beg, persuade, and threaten to get the right to buy clothes."[14] Once they were able to persuade one or two designers, he continues, the others followed. That they had to cajole designers to sell them garments underscored Mr. Johnson's conclusion that designers feared how their current clientele might respond to seeing the garments on black bodies. It also mirrored the racism that black consumers faced in U.S. department stores during the show's early years.[15] The highly closed world of high fashion revolved around

John and Eunice Johnson wedding party, 1942

Left to right: Eunice, John, and Gertrude Johnson, owners of Johnson Publishing Company, 1965

exclusivity of access and, at the time, a specific African American consumer market had not been articulated let alone included among the exclusive purchasers of luxury goods. By the early 1960s, however, Mrs. Johnson was beginning to make a name for herself as a serious purchaser of couture. Her ability to access the latest in European fashion is reflected in her fashion columns for *Ebony* as well as the ever-expanding list of designers noted in the traveling show's programs. During the 1960s, numerous cover spreads appeared dedicated to promoting a particular year's Fashion Fair theme featuring Mrs. Johnson's buying trips, the models traveling with the show, and highlighting ensembles that audiences could expect to see if they purchased a ticket.[16]

If the 1960s were about Mrs. Johnson's expanding access, the 1970s were about solidifying her place in the world of high fashion and expanding the reach of the Ebony Fashion Fair. Johnson continued her travel to the fashion houses of Europe and New York, deepening relationships with design houses and shaping the traveling show into one where audience members expected to see the latest fashions. Throughout the decade, Mrs. Johnson purchased some of the more iconic pieces in fashion for her audiences and the show itself grew dramatically. In 1976, the show grew to a two-part season and nearly 150 shows. Fashion Fair had become an established part of the cultural landscape for African Americans to raise funds for their charitable interests, whether a sorority or another volunteer organization.

Ebony Fashion Fair was characterized not just by the caliber and diversity of the fashion it showcased but the style with which Fashion Fair models displayed the clothing. Fashion Fair was never simply a runway show; instead, viewers enjoyed a multisensory experience featuring music, dancing, and a stylized presentation of fabulous fashion. After all, its goal was not just to showcase fashion; it was also an entertainment showcase, a promotion for Johnson publications, and a fundraiser. While fashion was the centerpiece, the show was crafted with those objectives in mind. Mrs. Johnson was critical in shaping the ways in which the show was executed and the ways in which the show grew.

While Mrs. Johnson extended her exclusive access to the closed-world of high fashion to her audiences, she also helped extend access to African Americans interested in participating in that world. Ebony Fashion Fair featured black designers from the show's earliest seasons and continued to do so throughout its history.

Ebony Fashion Fair model Harish Pandya during the 1971 season

In some early programs, "negro" designers were signaled out but as time went on, black designers were included with the list of American designers in the show's program. Since African American designers rarely had the access or financial backing to participate in traditional runway shows, those interested in having their designs featured in the traveling show sent their sketches directly to the Fashion Fair offices at Johnson Publishing. If selected, Mrs. Johnson purchased directly from them. Likewise, features of established and up-and-coming black designers appeared in *Ebony*. As with mainstream designers, Mrs. Johnson had favorite African American designers, including Stephen Burrows, Rufus Barkley, and Patrick Kelly, from whom she regularly purchased.

While Ebony Fashion Fair promoted African American designers, perhaps its most significant legacy was showcasing black models. Most black models who acquired any type of fame and recognition in the 1950s through the 1980s appeared in the pages of *Ebony* or on the cover of the Fashion Fair program. High-profile models such as Pat Cleveland, Beverly Johnson, Mounia, and Iman, among others, were featured in print, but a unique aspect of the Ebony Fashion Fair was the way in which models for the touring show were selected. The show's touring models weren't agency models; instead, Johnson recruited through the pages of *Ebony* and *Jet*, printing height specifications and extending an open invitation to women and men who thought they had what it took to be an Ebony Fashion Fair model. If an aspiring model's application and photograph piqued Mrs. Johnson's interest, the applicant was flown to Chicago to audition in front of a panel of Ebony Fashion Fair staff members, including both of the Johnsons. Thus, a young person from Small Town, America, had a chance of wearing some of the world's finest garments and touring the country to display them. This access to the world of fashion modeling mirrored the access the Ebony Fashion Fair provided its audiences.

As producer and director of the traveling show, Eunice Johnson was ultimately responsible for all aspects of crafting what and who her audiences saw. From her very involved selection of each season's ensembles to the men and women on whom those ensembles were displayed, she made clear choices based on her own ideas of what was fashionable and stylish as well as insight into what would resonate with Ebony Fashion Fair audiences. She shaped a show that,

Eunice Johnson working with a young designer and model, 1972

Eunice Johnson with designer Yves Saint Laurent, 1972

Eunice Johnson with models during the thirty-third annual Fashion Fair, 1991

in many ways, reflected the style stories she authored for *Ebony*. She did so with full knowledge of the critical place of fashion within larger society but also with the knowledge that Ebony Fashion Fair was as much about the projection and reflection of possibilities as it was about fashion. Further, Mrs. Johnson never lost sight of the philanthropic aspect of the show stating, in a 2009 interview, that Ebony Fashion Fair was an opportunity for her to give back to the community some of what had been given to her.

Ebony Fashion Fair projected ideals of success, accomplishment, and aspiration—all critical to Johnson Publishing Company's mission. In many ways, the show used fashion as a means of showing black women what was possible. Certainly, this was the case in the traveling fashion show's earliest days. As the Johnsons were demanding to be included in the closed world of high fashion, African Americans were asserting their place in other areas of society. The traveling show, like *Ebony* and *Jet* magazines, painted a picture of possibility and the material attainment that accompanied success. And, as the material possibilities for African Americans grew, so did the traveling show.

Ebony Fashion Fair was also about the audiences who attended and the sponsors who used the show to further their own philanthropic missions. In its fifty-year history, the fashion show raised tens of millions of dollars for black charitable organizations, including the United Negro College Fund. Ebony Fashion Fair was a spectacle of performance, a top-rate fashion show, and part of the promotion of a business enterprise that addressed an ignored and underserved market. Much like the family of Johnson publications, it never took for granted that people, especially those invisible or problematically portrayed within dominant culture, long to see the best possible visions of themselves.

NOTES

1. Johnson, John H., with Lerone Bennet, Jr. *Succeeding Against the Odds: The Autobiography of a Great American Businessman.* (New York: Amistad, 1992), 248–252. Mr. Johnson recounts the beginning of the Ebony Fashion Fair traveling show in his autobiography. Johnson viewed the show as a business opportunity and pursued it as such.
2. Ibid, 248.
3. A November 1958 issue of the *Chicago Defender* states that the traveling show made its debut in the city that year. Chicago was one of thirty locations to which Ebony Fashion Fair traveled. The show was held in the Grand Ballroom of the Conrad Hilton Hotel.
4. John Johnson was very transparent about his approach to publishing magazines. Whenever he found "a magazine with strong Black readership, I brought out a Black counterpart." Johnson, 206.
5. Green, Adam. *Selling the Race: Culture, Community, and Black Chicago, 1940–1955.* (Chicago: University of Chicago Press, 2007), 142.
6. Ibid., 156.
7. For much of the twentieth century, the dominant images of black womanhood were the Mammy and the Jezebel. Diametric opposites, the mammy's image centers on her place as a laborer devoid of femininity and sexuality while the Jezebel image rests on the idea of the sexually available black woman.
8. Perhaps no other story exemplifies this interruption as much as the 1955 murder of Chicago teen Emmett Till. John Johnson struggled with featuring the brutal images of Till's remains in *Jet*. The issue sold out immediately and documented an important moment in the Civil Rights Movement.
9. Ibid., 142.
10. Ibid., 141–142. Green examined the ways in which John Johnson and *Ebony*'s first editor, Ben Burns, addressed readers' questions about the magazine's title. In one of his responses, John Johnson argued that blackness is something in which to take pride and that it's a color of high esteem. The magazine title celebrated that blackness.
11. Johnson, 120.
12. Ibid., 159.
13. John Johnson references Eunice Johnson constantly in his autobiography. He does state that she did not always work full-time for the company; this changed with her involvement in Fashion Fair (fashion show, fashion feature, and later the cosmetic line). Mrs. Johnson was responsible for locating the building at 1820 South Michigan Avenue and the South Loop lot they occupied until June 2012.
14. Ibid., 252.
15. In many instances, African American shoppers could not try on clothes or accessories in department stores. They were forced to buy the merchandise and try it on at home, meaning that all items were final sale.
16. The October 1963 cover of *Ebony* featured Fashion Fair models in garments to be featured in the upcominig season.

Maxine Leeds Craig

RESPECT AND PLEA

The Meaning of Sty

I GREW UP READING *Ebony* and usually started from the back. When my family's copy arrived in the mail, after a glance at the cover I would flip the magazine over to go directly to the fashion section where I could find brown-skinned models in clothes more enchanting and forward thinking than anything I could see in downtown Brooklyn. There were three-piece ensembles for sleeping, gowns trimmed with feathers, and outfits in which every element, including the boxy-heeled shoe, opaque hosiery, eccentrically geometric coat, and wide-brimmed hat, were the same dazzling shade of pumpkin. At a time when wearing pants to public school would have triggered a trip to the principal's office, *Ebony* showed me an elegant model wearing culottes, which took the popular midi-length dress and fused it with the then bold idea of wearing pants. *Ebony* delivered the glamour of a distant fashion world to readers like me across the country.

Fashion had a regular place in *Ebony* because style has had an enduringly important place in African American life. This essay explores the reasons why African Americans paid attention to dress in the past, and why clothing continues to be an essential vehicle for contemporary collective and individual black expression. African Americans used clothes to say, in different eras, what it meant to be Negro, colored, black, or African. The very humanity of African Americans was negated by enslavement. After emancipation routine assaults to black rights and dignity continued unabated. Knowing that respect would rarely be freely given, black men and women used clothes to have some control over how they would be perceived.

Clothing, however, was never just about commanding respect. Dressing up was also a source of pleasure. The ability to improvise, to think on one's feet and make creative magic in the moment, is highly valued across realms of African American culture. Improvisation is not about making something from nothing. On the contrary, it is a capacity that rests upon having such a confident command of one's instrument, language, game, or material that one can appear to effortlessly create something unique on the spot. Jazz music, spectacular play on the basketball court, double dutch, and hip-hop are manifestations of skilled African American improvisation. The ability to use the materials at hand to make something new is a key component of the aesthetics that informed black style.

Black men and women designed clothing and assembled outfits that flaunted the ability to find just the right place between fitting in and standing out. But which group did they seek to fit in to, and against whom did they wish to stand out? The place of dress in African American life is as complicated as black identity. That is to say, while there is certainly something identifiable as a distinctive national black culture, there has never been an entirely homogenous black experience. African American communities were, and continue to be, complex entities, continually transformed by migration and social and political change, and structured by differences in economic position, generational aspiration, religious affiliation, and sexual identity. At any moment there is not one black style, but many, corresponding to the manifold ways of being black.

CLOTHING AND RESPECT

Historians Shane White and Graham White have shown that since being brought to American shores in the eighteenth century, and regardless of the availability of resources, African Americans have used clothing as a way to assert autonomy and claim respect. Even while enduring the unspeakably harsh conditions of slavery, African Americans artfully assembled available secondhand clothing and used natural dyes and the sewing techniques of quilting and patchwork to make decorative clothing by hand. Emancipation ended slavery but most African Americans were emancipated into dire poverty and environments that relentlessly assaulted their rights, safety, and dignity. Denial of respect to African Americans was central to a white supremacist order that lasted in its most extreme forms through the middle of the twentieth century. Throughout the nation discrimination in employment confined the vast

Fashion Fair feature, *Ebony*, September 1968

majority of African Americans to low-wage, menial work. Segregation in housing was tolerated and even supported by government policies until the Civil Rights Movement won the enactment of anti-discrimination legislation. Restricted to housing in persistently devalued neighborhoods, African Americans were thereby excluded from the route many whites traveled towards upward mobility. In the southern states blacks faced pervasive, infinite forms of social degradation. Social codes, enforced by legal and extra-legal violence, demanded black subordination to whites in every interpersonal interaction. These codes were tied to a belief system that restricted honor to whites. Blacks were ceaselessly disrespected through forms of disparagement that had particularly gendered and sexual dimensions. In racist speech, writing, and imagery, black men and women were depicted by whites as ugly, uncouth, asexual, or hypersexual. Grotesque caricature was used to defend and perpetuate racial segregation and the violation of black civil rights. While the forms that racism took in the North were usually less directly supported by local law, less violent, and more covert, African Americans who moved from the South to the North still lived lives shaped by enduring patterns of discrimination. Wherever they lived, African Americans were psychically assaulted by a changing array of disparaging representations of blacks in popular culture.

When black men and women stepped out into a society dominated by whites, they carried themselves into places where their value was likely to be threatened. Dress was a way to ward off that threat. They therefore "dressed up." Wearing clothes that expressed self-care was a way to demand the respect that could not be taken for granted. Dress was a way to assert one's high value in public, regardless of economic position. In the late nineteenth century and early part of the twentieth century African American community leaders were explicit about using dress as a way to assert the dignity of the race. Often framed in terms of "race uplift," the responsibility to attend to one's appearance for the collective good of the race was particularly impressed upon women, who were taught that the elevation of the race depended upon the character of the women, and that character would be evaluated by appearance. Black leaders exhorted women to deport themselves with dignity because the race had to defend itself against the slurs of white racists. Their belief was that black women who dressed well would be walking demonstrations of the decency and good worth of all black people.

Such concern regarding appearance might be dismissed as the view of an elite group which was out of touch with the majority of black women. There were indeed tensions between some middle-class blacks in northern cities and their poorer neighbors, many of whom were recent migrants from the rural South. Yet these class tensions must be put in perspective. At the beginning of the twentieth century, few among the black middle class would have been considered elites on a national scale. Furthermore the black middle class had myriad interpersonal connections to poor blacks. Occupational, residential, and commercial segregation meant that their relative wealth and status was built either through businesses that catered to African Americans or from occupations such as teaching which, while not menial, were not particularly lucrative.

The message that a carefully styled appearance would provide black women better lives was also promoted by black hair-care and fashion entrepreneurs. Annie Turnbo Malone and Madam C. J. Walker built highly successful businesses by developing and marketing hair care products for black women. They developed beauty-care franchise enterprises that provided black women with opportunities to gain some measure of autonomy by going into business for themselves. Black hair-care entrepreneurs promoted their products through advertisements that disseminated the message that black women could improve their lives through attention to appearance. This message invited all black women to claim femininity and beauty as qualities that were accessible and rightfully theirs. Many black women who labored in occupations that garnered little respect outside of black communities were receptive to the message that dignity could be claimed through personal actions, even if that message came from the black elite or from magazine advertisements. They were attentive to appearance and, if in their workdays had to wear a dreary uniform or simple work clothes, would seize the opportunity to dress as well as possible when on their own time.

DEFINING BLACK STYLE

The question remains, what did it mean to dress well? While a broad spectrum of African Americans agreed that dressing well was both important and pleasurable, there was inevitably considerable generational, class, and regional variation in African American tastes in

Formal studio portraits of James E. Jones (top) and Jennie Waring (bottom).
The responsibility to attend to one's appearance for the collective good of the race was particularly impressed upon women. Chicago History Museum. ICHi-22360 and ICHi-22382.

clothing. Early twentieth-century race leaders used clothing to demonstrate through appearance that they were no different than whites. However the denial of racial difference was not always the intended effect of African American style. Many African Americans dressed to meet standards that circulated within their own communities. These standards may have had only a tenuous relationship to whatever was stylish among whites. Black style was nurtured in spaces where no whites were present, in churches where for women a hat was required and a handheld fan a necessity. Black style flourished in juke joints and dance palaces where a well-designed dress or suit was one that facilitated movement. Beauty advice was gained in black beauty parlors and in home kitchens where black women straightened each other's hair to form styles that were never identical to and therefore not merely imitative of white women's hair. When black women styled their hair, their immediate models were other black women. The wearing of clothes and performance of style always takes place in local settings. It is a show put on for familiar people. Personal style was flaunted on sidewalks where the arbiters of taste lived within walking distance.

Yet while women shopped, sewed, and dressed locally, they saw images of beauty and fashion produced far away. In the first half of the twentieth century, the vast majority of mass-media images of blacks took the form of disparaging caricatures created by whites for white audiences. These images typically represented black men and women as poorly dressed servants, or in a particularly vicious form of satire, as buffoons who made themselves ridiculous by dressing above their station in life. Within black communities such imagery was countered to some extent by a range of media aimed at black audiences. African American Studies scholar Noliwe Rooks has shown that as far back as 1891, African American women published magazines in which African American women were represented as beautiful and fashionable. The first of these was *Ringwood's Afro-American Journal of Fashion*. Like most of the small number of black women's magazines that would follow it in the first half of the twentieth century, *Ringwood's* went out of business within a few years of its debut. Black newspapers were more numerous than magazines, and many were highly successful ventures that reached large numbers of readers nationwide. They included a limited amount of visual imagery, which often took the form of portraits. In the 1920s and 1930s, African Americans could see images of fashionable black people, in what were known as "race films." Some of these films were produced by white-owned studios, but others by black filmmakers, like Oscar Micheaux, whose melodramas featured glamorous African American women. All sought to cater to black audiences who attended segregated movie houses or mainstream venues that showed films to blacks at less popular times of day.

In the post–World War II era, African Americans began to have access to a wider array of images of black celebrities. The proliferation and dissemination of these images and the eventual slow decline of stereotyped media caricatures was no accident. Black journalists and civil rights organizations had protested racist imagery in media for decades. Their efforts began to have results in the 1960s. At the same time, black journalists and fashion and entertainment entrepreneurs successfully created magazines, fashion shows, beauty contests, and modeling agencies that would provide venues to display black beauty and talent. They were business people seeking to make money doing creative work, but they were also establishing black institutions or integrating formerly white institutions and thereby contributed to dismantling the structures of racism.

BLACK STYLE AND DISTANT FASHION

Appearing for the first time in 1945, *Ebony* was a major component of the new black media of the postwar era. *Ebony* reached black homes across the country and contributed to the formation of a national black culture. The magazine's outlook was upbeat. It was a monthly showcase of black achievement. Though its politics evolved along with the rapid changes of the ensuing decades, *Ebony*'s editors primarily advocated for the inclusion of blacks in formerly white institutions, a political orientation that expressed itself through its pages, including those devoted to fashion. The most successful positions within the fashion and entertainment industries had been closed to black women. *Ebony*'s fashion section featured brown-skinned women dressed in the clothing of Europe's top designers. These

Fashion Fair feature, *Ebony*, November 1959

photographs were visible proof that black women could be every bit as glamorous as the white models featured in the nation's dominant media.

Style is local but high fashion's allure often relies on distance. In the American imagination of the 1950s, no place was as fashionable as Paris, and nowhere as glamorous as the French Riviera. Writing in November 1959, *Ebony*'s fashion editor Freda DeKnight told readers "the latest in fashion is still wrapped in the phrase 'a Paris original'." DeKnight went on shopping trips in Europe to find clothes that were the height of fashion for *Ebony*'s Fashion Fair. In 1959, readers were shown those clothes worn by white models photographed in

Europe but were given the message that equivalent glamour was within the reach of African American women. High fashion may be distant, but local women could be as stylish as Parisians. DeKnight let Ebony readers in on the secret. "The budget-minded housewife will not have to worry," she wrote. "Copies of many of the finest are available for less than $50." Each month DeKnight's pages struck that sort of balance. She presented a fantasy world of distant glamour, located in Europe, but then shrunk the distance between the lives of her readers and that world. Fashion relied on distant places to establish its authority and allure. In the 1950s, high fashion had to be from Paris or Italy. *Ebony*'s staff traveled there and brought it home, but then gave legitimacy to copies and encouraged home-sewn adaptations. Inspired by the fashions displayed in *Ebony*, mothers and daughters could go to the local fabric store, browse the bolts of cloth, find a pattern that translated high fashion into a doable project, and make their own versions at home. They held neighborhood fashion shows, crowned each other in schoolyard beauty contests, and looked beautiful in church.

As a publication written intentionally to showcase black achievement, *Ebony* promoted a vision of African American life that was fully integrated into the American dream. That dream was populated by nuclear families in which industrious, non-working wives stretched pennies to buy copies of the finest dresses or used Simplicity patterns to stitch homemade versions. *Ebony* built bridges between the fantasy and the achievable. Between the pages of a 1959 photo spread of white European models wearing Chantilly lace, the editors placed an ad for Dixie Peach hair pomade featuring "famous colored models" from "New York's leading model agency." The ad showed aspirational little girls that black women could be models too. By 1960, the models shown in *Ebony*'s fashion section were black.

Travel itself was an important part of *Ebony*'s vision of the good life. In 1960, a time when black people could not ride in the front of an interstate bus or even swim in many local pools, when the cost of an airplane trip was beyond reach and stewardesses were always white because the standards of beauty held by airline personnel departments categorically excluded blacks, *Ebony* posed black models holding Pan Am flight bags and standing in front of travel posters of Scotland, Paris, Spain and Mexico. "Since vacations today usually involve travel" they told readers, women needed luscious cashmere for those cool evenings aboard cruise ships. These fantasies were inviting and plausible because of the era's optimism. None of it would be handed to African Americans, but through protest, strategy, and creativity the formerly impossible seemed within grasp.

In the late 1950s, the few black women who worked as professional models had extremely limited opportunities and were underpaid in comparison to their white counterparts. Determined to change this situation, some ambitious black women began to create an infrastructure to make it possible for black women to have more lucrative careers as models. Ophelia DeVore was one of the most successful of these entrepreneurs. As shown by historian Malia McAndrews, DeVore strategically traveled to Europe with her models in order to open doors for them back at home. DeVore recognized that in the American mind, Europe was the source of high fashion. By taking her models to the perceived center of the fashion world, she associated them with the fascination that adhered to places like the French Riviera. Some of DeVore's models achieved notable successes overseas. While post–World War II France was hardly a racial paradise, its different demographics and history meant that the French fashion world was willing to celebrate a few American black women as exotic beauties. DeVore's models returned to the United States bearing the distinction of having been celebrated as beauties by the most prestigious European arbiters of taste. They were able to leverage that prestige at home, where in the 1960s U.S. corporations, prodded by the demands of civil rights organizations, and beginning to recognize the value of advertising to black consumers, began to hire brown-skinned models.

Having won success for black models in some of the most elite circles, and after parlaying those victories into viable modeling careers for a small group of professional black models, DeVore opened the Ophelia DeVore School of Modeling and Charm to make the techniques of modeling accessible to ordinary women. During the 1950s and 1960s "charm" schools were common in the United States. These schools taught young women make-up techniques and forms of embodiment—ways of sitting and walking—that were defined as ladylike. Charm schools promoted the belief that middle-class forms of feminine deportment were foundational for both success and self-esteem. Within black communities these schools can be seen as extensions of the efforts made by early twentieth-century black community leaders to promote the adoption of the appearance of respectability. By the 1950s and 1960s however, the image of feminine respectability had evolved into a form of embodiment that was a bit sexier. It involved short skirts and stiletto heels and the knowledge of how to get in and out of a car wearing them. The embodiment they promoted was simultaneously hyperfeminine and respectable. It was the same aesthetic promoted by Berry Gordy as he groomed and trained groups like the Supremes. Part of why pointy boots, slender pants, and a black turtleneck sweater will always look good to me is because I saw that image every time I picked up my Supremes A-Go-Go album so that I could dance to "Love is Like An Itching in My Heart" one more time. A generation of women learned a lot about fashion from the Supremes.

BLACK STYLE AND AFRICA

Wherever she lived, whatever she believed, whether she was an activist or not, any black woman who lived in the United States in the 1960s and 1970s was affected by the political, social, economic and cultural change produced by the Civil Rights and Black Power movements. Particularly for youth, the days of aspiring to respectability ended rapidly. Respect, not respectability was what mattered. Youth rejected the desire for respectability. Some rejected signifiers of wealth and exclusivity. They proudly wore styles such as black leather jackets that were associated with political militancy and sought out fabrics and designs that proclaimed their identification with the African continent. Style is referential. It points to places and identities. Before the 1960s, Europe represented the epitome of fashion for the middle classes, and hardly anyone in the United States, regardless of class or race, consciously identified Africa as important to her aesthetic. In the late 1960s the rise of independent black African nations, and the desire to embrace and celebrate black identity made Africa a new source of cultural inspiration for blacks living in the United States. People who had seen themselves as Negro or colored began to identify as black, African American, or African, turn away from European cultural orientations, and looked to Africa for inspiration regarding ritual, art, hair-care techniques, and fashion. Shops began to appear in black neighborhoods that made African fabrics, dashikis, and wooden carved hair picks available for purchase. Women learned African techniques of tying head wraps and braiding, and incorporated these styles into their daily lives.

This change in orientation registered to some degree in *Ebony*'s fashion pages. A 1968 issue noted the "Afro-Asian influences that have been creeping into men's fashions for the past two or three years. While their most extreme expressions will be in the dashikis, togas and boubous worn by 'roots' -seeking black-awareness ideologues, the eye-dazzling colors, the bold, soulful prints of Africa will also enliven less ethnic oriented men's wear." In subsequent years, Africa as a source of inspiration appeared occasionally in *Ebony*'s fashion pages, and in most instances was presented without reference to ideology. For example African jewelry might be placed atop a western style evening gown. Nonetheless Europe continued as the most common glamorous reference point of the fashion pages.

In the everyday life of black communities the popularity of styles, such as boxy dashiki shirts and large Afros, waned to such a degree that they have become humorous symbols of a bygone era. Nonetheless elements of an aesthetic that is inspired by Africa have become permanent parts of an expanded African American sense of style. Intricate braids, kente cloth, and other African fabrics have become enduring components of contemporary black style.

CONTEMPORARY BLACK STYLE

Any attempt to describe a singular black aesthetic would obscure the complexity of black communities. Though it would be a mistake to speak of a singular black aesthetic, it would be just as erroneous to ignore the existence of a dynamic, evolving, and distinctively black set of orientations toward and tastes regarding clothing and bodily adornment. Popular African American aesthetics regarding both men's and women's clothing continue to exist in dialogue with, but distinct from, mainstream fashion. Often black style has meant an appreciation of a wider range of colors for women's as well as men's clothing than whites would wear. African Americans have enjoyed formal clothing, and displayed a willingness to dress up, at times and places when whites broadly adopted informality. Many contemporary black women

"Men's Wear: Afro Asian," *Ebony*, September 1968

enjoy the creative possibilities inherent in hair and nail extensions at a time when white women tend to use beauty products to create an appearance of naturalness.

Those most concerned with favorably impressing whites adhere more closely to mainstream tastes. And apart from any inherent pleasure that may be gained by dressing up, white assumption of black criminality pressures African Americans, especially men, to avoid casual clothing. Thus clothing continues to matter in black life in ways that it has never had to matter to whites. At the extreme, wearing the wrong clothing can place a black man's life at risk. In environments in which clothing is richly symbolic, the act of dressing becomes a way of entering into a highly charged political field. Wearing a hoodie or sagging pants can be a way of proclaiming one's position in relation to demands to be compliant. Yet at a time when celebrities wear sagging pants, black youths may wear defiant-looking clothing with no more political intent than the desire to blend in with their peers.

The fashion world is in some respects more inclusive than it was when Ophelia DeVore had to take her models to the pinnacle of Europe's fashion scene before they could gain less glamorous work selling food products in print advertisements at home. Black models are a common presence in many clothing catalogs. Still, anachronistically, certain popular U.S. brands of clothing continue to seek to define themselves through the use of exclusively white models and salespersons, and have only abandoned such strategies when taken to court. High fashion uses black models in a limited way, sporadically including black models for a particular kind of look, in ways that do not displace whiteness as the beauty norm. Few black designers receive significant financial backing. Yet black style in everyday life continues to be a source of pleasure, a practice of self- and collective definition, and a source of inspiration for trend seekers beyond black communities.

FOR FURTHER READING

Craig, Maxine Leeds. *Ain't I a Beauty Queen: Black Women, Beauty and the Politics of Race*. (New York: Oxford University Press, 2002).

   From the beginning of the twentieth century to the emergence of Black is Beautiful, Craig chronicles the intertwining of politics and beauty standards in African American life.

Haidarali, Laila. "Polishing Brown Diamonds: African American Women, Popular Magazines, and the Advent of Modeling in Early Postwar America." *Journal of Women's History* 17(1) (2005): 10–37.

   Haidarali traces the beginnings of opportunities for brown-skinned models to the expansion of corporate marketing to African Americans in the post-World War II era.

Kaiser, Susan B. and Sarah Rebolloso McCullough. "Entangling the Fashion Subject Through the African Diaspora: From Not to (K)not in Fashion Theory." *Fashion Theory: The Journal of Dress, Body & Culture* 14 (3) (2010): 361–386.

   These authors show that African American style can only be understood by transcending binary thinking.

McAndrew, Malia. "A Twentieth-Century Triangle Trade: Selling Black Beauty at Home and Abroad, 1945–1965." *Enterprise & Society* 11(4) (2010): 784–810.

   This article provides a detailed account and analysis of how Ophelia DeVore's transnational strategy established a place for black models in fashion and advertising.

O'Neal, Gwendolyn S. "The African American Church, its Sacred Cosmos and Dress," in *Religion, Dress and the Body*, ed. Linda B. Arthur. (New York: Berg Publishers, 1999), 117–134.

   O'Neal identifies the importance of The Black Church as an institution that preserves and nurtures African American culture including black aesthetics regarding dress.

Rooks, Noliwe. *Hair Raising: Beauty, Culture, and African American Women*. (New Brunswick: Rutgers University Press, 1996).

   This is a history of the way in which the politics and practice of black beauty culture were shaped by black women entrepreneurs like Madam C. J. Walker.

Rooks, Noliwe. *Ladies' Pages: African American Women's Magazines and the Culture That Made Them*. (New Brunswick: Rutgers University Press, 2004).

   Rooks uncovers the little known history of black women's magazines, which existed as far back as 1891, and describes the way in which fashion was promoted as a tool for defining African American women's identity.

White, Shane and Graham White. *Stylin': African American Expressive Culture from Its Beginnings to the Zoot Suit*. (Ithaca: Cornell University Press, 1998).

   Drawing on sources ranging from escaped slave notices to oral history, this book provides a detailed history of African American personal style.

Virginia Heaven

THE POWER OF FASHION

WHAT IS FASHION?

THE APPAREL INDUSTRY is colossal and employs millions of people across the globe. It encompasses a vast array of products ranging from budget to luxury apparel and accessories, and every price point in-between. But what is "fashion"? There are so many conflicting definitions for the meaning of fashion that it is seemingly in-definable. It manifests as the practical to the practically un-wearable. It is regarded by some who consider themselves "fashionable" as a vehicle for daily self-expression, and by others who have no interest in fashion merely as comfortable body-covering. Long regarded as frippery and lightweight study in the academy, in recent decades it has been regarded more seriously. In actual fact, fashion gains much of its importance and power from its role in defining an era, by historically representing the milieu and social mores of a society. Who can think of the 1920s without conjuring an image of a woman dancing in a classic flapper dress from the mid-decade? But, for all that fashion denotes to those that wear and follow it, or despise and eschew it, we all participate in it in some way whether we want to or not.

In 2011, the global apparel, accessories and luxury goods market value was $1,778.5 billion, with a growth of 4.3 percent[2] in a recessive economy. Fashion nowadays

Ebony Fashion Fair

is about making money; it's a very savvy wolf in sheep's clothing that changes seasonally. This of course is nothing new. Historically there is ample evidence that fashion as we know it really emerged with the growing middle-classes in the Middle Ages as an outward, and easily interpreted sign of rising through society's ranks. The Industrial Revolution literally manufactured a new era of prosperity and a burgeoning upper middle-class who craved visible signals of social advancement. Thus by the middle of the nineteenth century the "dress-for-success" maxim became increasingly formalized. Charles Frederick Worth (1826–95) became the first official couturier; he seized his moment to solidify the role of fashion as a social signifier in 1858 Paris. Worth clearly recognized that fashion is essentially scaffolded by commerce and driven by the upwardly mobile; more importantly he understood that creating a recognizable brand was essential to success. Worth knew that high fashion had as much to do with outstanding customer service and exclusivity, as with superb design and excellent workmanship. Certainly dressmakers of note had been dressing the affluent and titled for centuries, but Worth managed to distill the concept of personal service into a potent cordial. In the following decades couture houses ebbed and flowed. In post–World War II Paris, almost a century after Worth, Christian Dior channeled and refined Worth's same approach for the modern era. He appeared to foresee and prepare for the approaching postwar boom, by adapting contemporary marketing methods to focus on fashion. Dior deployed strategies that both anticipated and then steered the discriminating fashion-conscious consumer. His daywear was divine; his evening wear was legendary. For the very wealthy he produced grand and luscious haute couture creations, conjuring mountains of silk taffeta and tulle embellished with thousands of beads and paillettes into remarkable breath-taking confections. But he also licensed copies of his designs to be made by selected stores at much lower cost. He diversified his product lines into perfume, hosiery, and accessories. Thus branded fashion was no longer the territory of the very rich; it had been seized and consumed by the growing middle-classes who appreciated designer labels and the concept of exclusivity, even if through a licensed copy. It should be noted that nowadays there are strict rules imposed on designers who wish to call themselves a couturier. Merely making beautiful clothes is not enough; the Paris Chamber of Commerce sets strict guidelines to preserve the designation and dignity of the brand 'haute couture'.

The century between these two grand masters had produced some of the most tumultuous changes in fashion history. Yet oddly, Dior's first collection and his New Look in 1947 had more in common with Worth's trussed

> *"Fashion implies a certain fluidity of the social structure of the community. There must be differences of social position, but it must seem possible and desirable to bridge these differences; in a ridgid hierarchy fashion is impossible."* —J. C. FLÜGEL[1]

and taxidermied nineteenth-century ladies, than the forward thinking fashion designers of the modernist 1920s and 1930s. Designers such as Gabrielle Chanel and Jean Patou broke new ground in fashion in the early decades of the twentieth century. Known for their sleek and boyish sportswear, their designs personified the new active woman that emerged after World War I. Dior, to all intents and purposes, took a step back in time, as fashion often does. The practical but mannish suits of the war years with their broad, padded shoulders and short skirts simply vanished and Dior's ultra-feminine silhouette took center stage. The softly rounded shoulders, nipped-in waist, and full, ankle-grazing skirts embodied high style and elegance. More important, it signaled the rebirth of haute couture and Paris as the fashion capital of the world. Dior was a great designer, but others at the time were equally as accomplished. What Dior managed to achieve, however, through a combination of skill, luck and timing was to instill his name into the public consciousness worldwide as the pinnacle of luxury and sartorial aspiration. Hence establishing his name as a powerful fashion brand was far more remarkable and revolutionary than anything he designed.

Although Paris had been established as the sun at the center of the fashion universe, there were other fashion centers emerging that would become very important in the following decades. After World War II, Italy was ready to give France a run for its money. Fashion historian Nicola White[3] proposed that the Marshall Plan helped jumpstart the Italian fashion industry as, "[the] United States of America played a vital role in the post-war evolution of Italian Fashion … through initial financial support and close involvement in the industrial organization of Italy … [also] as a supplier of progressive manufacturing methods … as a cultural model … [and] as a keen market." Prior to the war, Italy boasted a thriving textile industry and fine dressmakers, but certainly not on the same scale as after the war. By the late 1950s, the Italian industry was firmly on its feet and, in addition, it was a friendly market to Americans.

Another fashion capital of importance was New York City, which had been the center of the fashion industry in the United States since the end of the nineteenth century. Apparel made in New York was typically mass-produced by thousands of garment workers who called the city their home. Collins[4] provides an overview of mass production and "section" work in factories that comprised sewing-machine operators making only one part of an overall garment. This method of production was much faster and cheaper since it eliminated the need to hire highly skilled seamstresses to construct an entire garment. As a result, attractive, inexpensive ready-to-wear clothing became available for the masses in the early twentieth century, which in turn boosted the need for high-end designers to establish more exclusive labels to dress the well-to-do. By the 1950s, designers such as Norman Norell, James Galanos, Bonnie Cashin, Claire McCadell, and Pauline Trigere were among those who first developed a distinctive American Style characterized by sleek, well edited, and beautifully realized high-fashion apparel.

Nothing much is different today, except that in the sixty plus years since World War II, many other centers known for their designers and manufacturing have expanded. Now much of the mass-produced clothing once made in Europe and America is made in Asia. Fashion now is truly part of the global economy. Most major fashion houses have a ready-to-wear line and haute couture rarely makes money, but serves mainly as an idea laboratory and a platform for marketing the brand. In Paris the bi-annual haute couture shows feature spring/summer and fall/winter collections, and in Italy the equivalent of haute couture known as Alta-Moda does the same. The ready-to-wear runway shows are also bi-annual and present the new styles for the coming season in a regular cycle, most notably in New York, London, Milan, and Paris. Nowadays, fashion is not just about apparel, it's also very much about marketing. Each season seemingly arbitrary design modifications can be powerful enough as to create seismic shifts, in what is perceived in the public consciousness as either in-style or outmoded. Fully harnessing the digital age, the fashion industry cues and reinforces social status by fashioning desire in apparel and accessories, through glossy ads featuring models starved to perfection and photoshopped into plasticity. In addition, celebrities (who are themselves marketed into myth) are carefully selected to be the 'spokesperson' for the brand and become part of the public signaling system. As a society, we are gorged on marketing campaigns, but when broken down into bite-sized pieces of information it is clear that branding is both a science and an art and so sophisticated as to be Machiavellian.

By simultaneously creating a desire and need for the new fashions and undermining confidence in the old styles, the trend machine successfully perpetuates a seemingly endless cycle of sartorial acquisition and disposal. When stated so baldly, fashion seems a *very* bad thing indeed. But John Carl Flügel, an early twentieth-century psychologist and author of *The Psychology of Clothes*,[5] did not think so. He argued that fashion is inextricably bound with social change and progression and symbolic of inherent human nature, "when, in psychological terms, one class begins seriously to aspire to the position of that above it, it is natural that the distinctive outward signs and symbols of the grades in question should become imprerilled [sic]." Flügel's theory suggests that as the lower rungs of society begin to move upward, they *need* the semiotics of dress to demonstrate their success. In turn, this awakened aspirational acquisition in the lower classes drives the already privileged classes to change their fashions frequently, just to ensure that they stay at least one step ahead of the *hoi polloi*. Perhaps then, we are just prosaic predictable creatures who are either displaying that we have already made it to the top of society's ladder, or alternatively, just attempting to look like we have.

But, if Flügel's compelling paradigm is applied to help deconstruct the incredible success of fifty years of Ebony Fashion Fair, it fits quite well. The Fashion Fair comprised some of the most glamorous, luxurious, and exclusive fashions of the era. The fact that the highest style was made available to a portion of society that was chronically underserved by entrenched, government-sanctioned racism, speaks of much more than merely abetting consumerism. In this case, when fashion becomes aspirational, it can be regarded as symbolic of the potential for upward mobility in the African American community.

EBONY FASHION FAIR

By the late 1950s, Johnson Publishing Company was a firmly established publishing empire. The Johnsons were well known in the African American community, and because traditionally people of rank and wealth were expected to practice philanthropy, the Johnsons were no exception. Ebony Fashion Fair began as a charity fundraiser in 1958. The show continued annually for five decades and rapidly expanded to include more apparel and venues each year. The audience of predominantly African American women came to see exclusive, beautiful, sensational and fantastic fashions; they were never disappointed. The ticket sales benefitted charity, but included in the price was a year's subscription to *Ebony* or six months of *Jet* magazine. Many laudable causes were funded during the run of the Fashion Fair, and the Johnsons utilized the opportunity for positive PR; it became a perfect blend of charity and commerce. Audiences in cities and towns, large and small, in auditoriums, theatres, and even high-school gymnasiums across America were able to see the very latest haute couture and ready-to-wear. Interestingly, it was practically impossible for *anyone* to see fashion of this quality. Even now, the couture shows are only open to the select few who either buy from or promote the design houses.

The very fact that Mrs. Johnson was buying from the premier fashion houses of Europe and America in the late 1950s is extraordinary. Nowadays we equate wealth with the capacity to open any doors, but the Johnsons as African Americans had to practically thrust themselves and their money into the ateliers. There are unsettling stories about the Johnsons' first attempts to purchase haute couture related to racial snubs. John H. Johnson recalls in in his autobiography: "It was necessary to overcome the fears and phobias of racism. When Eunice [Mrs. Johnson] and I went to Europe with Freda [DeKnight, the first producer and director of the show] for the first time to buy clothes, we had to beg, persuade, and threaten to get the right to buy clothes. Certain designers assumed that White women wouldn't value their designs if they were worn by Black women. We

Fabrice, 1990
Matching ensembles for woman and man; in Ebony Fashion Fair tradition, the male models' primary role was to escort and highlight the female models' ensembles.

finally got through to one or two of the leading designers, and the others followed."[6] The Johnsons' daughter Linda Johnson Rice, chairman of Johnson Publishing Company, reinforced this by explaining that attitudes only began to change when it eventually became clear that her mother "wasn't begging or borrowing, she was buying."[7]

So, even though it was difficult to do business at first, Mrs. Johnson gradually established a reputation for a connoisseur's eye that was underscored by Johnson Publishing Company's deep pockets. Though JPC wrote the checks for the apparel, Mrs. Johnson was the creative force behind the show from its earliest days, going on buying trips to France and Italy starting in 1958. The buying trips for the Fashion Fair show are documented in *Ebony* magazine and, from the 1960s onward, in the programs too. It is also evident from the programs that the Italian designers seem take precedence over the French, though as the Fashion Fair progressed over the years the number of French designers increased. Perhaps one of the reasons that Italian designers were favored was that, as previously explained it was a much newer market, designers were friendly to American buyers and eager to make sales. However, Mrs. Johnson is purported to have driven a hard bargain when purchasing for the Fashion Fair. This was reinforced by Audrey Smalz, commentator for Ebony Fashion Fair from 1970 until 1977 and associate buyer for the Fashion Fair.[8] Ms. Smalz accompanied Mrs. Johnson on many buying trips and commented that part of the reason Italy was preferred, was related to the fact that the Italians were more willing to come to a more satisfactory arrangement on the price.

MRS. JOHNSON AS A CURATOR OF FASHION

In 1964, the Ebony Fashion Fair program transformed from a pamphlet into a booklet, and Mrs. Johnson wrote a fashion editorial that provided a short overview for the season's fashion. She also often explained how the title of the current year's show evolved. It makes for fascinating reading because not only is she right on point with her descriptions of the prevailing trends of the day, she also makes it evident she is looking for the next big thing, "I always look for the trend-setters," she said. "I don't have to be concerned about whether an item is going to sell, or if I can get reorders. I want showstoppers that will look terrific on the runway, and I want fashions that will forecast what's on the way in, not just what's selling and being worn now."⁹ From the final assemblage of apparel, the storyline for the Fashion Fair would evolve; the selections appear to be carefully calibrated to work as a cohesive statement in each section. In 1964, for example the show was entitled, *Ebony Fashion Fair with a Spanish Flair*; the program promised the audience "a background of plot and mystery— a story of international intrigue and romance, just for fun."¹⁰ Evidently, even from the earliest years the entertainment aspect of the fashion show was just as important as the clothing. In many respects Mrs. Johnson's role as the director and producer of Ebony Fashion Fair can be compared to that of a curator. Curatorial practice is largely associated with museums and galleries, but one major aspect of a curator's work is the selection and display of cultural artifacts. In museums, curators combine scholarship with entertainment. Often the primary role of curators is to provide the rationale for collecting, the interpretation of objects and the explication for an exhibition. Similarly, every year Mrs. Johnson assessed and evaluated the trends from the thousands of garments she viewed on the haute couture and ready-to-wear runways in Europe and America. From thousands of items she edited it down to approximately 180–200 ensembles, or exits, as they are known in the fashion industry. The final group represented the season's style zeitgeist curated specifically for her Ebony Fashion Fair audience.

The Johnsons made a study of African American consumers and their buying power; their business success was based on understanding and marketing to their target audience. Examples of this attention to the customer profile feature in an interesting article in the 1967 Fashion Fair program, *Fashion Rebellion*, entitled, *The New Negro Woman-An Urban Trendsetter*. The article quotes compelling statistics, "U. S. government figures show that you as an urban Negro woman buyer spend approximately seventy per cent more for quality fashionable clothing and accessories than other women in the same income class."¹¹ The statistics support the idea that African American women were interested in and attentive to their appearance. Aware that the majority of their audience lacked the financial resources to purchase the highly priced apparel featured in Ebony Fashion Fair, Mrs. Johnson referred to other alternatives. An article in *Ebony* in 1959 entitled The Magic of a Paris Original, states "price tags run up to $1,500. But the budget-minded housewife will not have to worry. Copies of many of the finest are available for less than $50."¹² To supplement the concept of obtaining copies, there were advertisements for fabric and also dressmaking patterns that appear with regularity in the show programs in the 1960s, 1970s, and 1980s. Hence Ebony Fashion Fair could also be considered as a vehicle for acknowledging and, perhaps, also shaping African American taste in fashion beyond the Fashion Fair runway.

Through the use of black models the show established something more; up until this point, models had been white. By using black models Mrs. Johnson transformed and accelerated the audience's connection to the fashion by proclaiming that to be black is to be not only beautiful, but also colorful, shapely, and identifiably fashionable. John H. Johnson recalled the phenomenon of using black models as a game-changer for black women, "The Ebony Fashion Show has also given Black America and the world a new concept of the kind of clothes Black women can wear. Before the Ebony Fashion Show, people said Black women couldn't wear red or yellow or purple. The fashion show proved that Black women could wear any color they wanted to wear. One of our earliest and best models, Terri Springer—tall, beautiful, shapely, and jet black—used to sashay across stages in spectacular colors that defined "Black is Beautiful before the phrase was invented."¹³ The cumulative effect of years of presenting high fashion to African Americans, on African Americans, with African American taste-making in mind, enabled Mrs. Johnson to be a change-agent who harnessed the power of fashion to reinforce positive cultural identity. A sidebar to this story is that in the 1991 Fashion Fair program, *Fashion with Passion*, there is an advertisement for Shani, Asha, and Nichelle, Mattel's glamorously dressed African American dolls. The ad proclaims "You told us you wanted features that reflected your child's natural beauty, with three different skin tones. You asked for clothes and jewelry in vibrant colors and designs— and we think you'll agree that these fashions are truly spectacular."¹⁴ The ad suggests and reinforces that the mainstream culture was finally waking up to the needs and desires of African Americans to see themselves in popular culture.

THE EXHIBITION SELECTIONS

Selected from more than 3,500 remaining pieces in the Ebony Fashion Fair fashion archive, the sixty-seven ensembles chosen for the exhibition *Inspiring Beauty: 50 years of Ebony Fashion Fair* clearly reveal that Mrs. Johnson had a flair for the glamorous, the luxurious, and the dramatic. The racks of alphabetized designers' gowns and ensembles resembled a pirate's booty of extraordinary fashion significance: Alaïa, Balestra, Balmain, Beene, Blass, Burrows, Cardin, Courrèges, Dior, Givenchy, Missoni, Miyake, de la Renta, Rucci, Saint Laurent, Ungaro, Valentino, Westwood, and many, many more. The garments resembled a congregation of practically everyone who has mattered in fashion for half a century. The collection also provided an overview of Mrs. Johnson's incredible ability to spot the most iconic pieces each year. Cordial and fruitful fashion relationships were formed with designers such as, Marc Bohan for the House of Dior, Hubert de Givenchy, Emanuel Ungaro, Yves Saint Laurent, Christian Lacroix at Jean Patou then under his own name, Fausto Sarli, Laura Biagiotti, Bill Blass, Oscar de la Renta, Bob Mackie and others. In several notable cases the collection held twenty or thirty pieces from a single designer that provided an edited document of their entire career. Moreover, in addition to the well-known and celebrated designers of Europe and America, Mrs. Johnson made it part of her mission to provide a platform for African American fashion designers who were rarely afforded the opportunities available to their white counterparts. So each year Mrs. Johnson would include examples of emerging and established African American designers including, Stephen Burrows, Rufus Barkley, Henry Jackson, Patrick Kelly, and Willi Smith.

As the consulting costume curator for the exhibition, my challenge was not what to include, but what to leave out! Over time things gradually began to fall into place, and medleys of different concepts were assembled. One of the grounding principles for deciding what to include was the theatricality factor. The show was essentially an entertainment phenomenon with music and dancing. One of the key criterions for Mrs. Johnson when she selected apparel for the Fashion Fairs, was how the clothes would look when they were in motion; the models' bodies and gestures transformed the clothes from ensembles into performance pieces. This aspect though crucial to the success of the live shows is obviously very difficult to display on mannequins. In addition, although there is some menswear in the show, the male models served largely as escorts to enhance and help present and set the scene for the beautifully clad female models.

Every year there was a focus on selecting garments in brilliant colors. In fact, there were five Ebony Fashion Fair shows over the years that referenced color in the title. The celebration of the body was another theme, and the collection had many examples of gorgeous gowns that revealed, and better yet revered the body. Luxurious fabrics and materials such as fur and feathers, embroidered and embellished surfaces were de rigueur. The total head-to-toe look was also present with ensembles that had custom-made hats and footwear. After months of evaluating multiple scenarios, the final choices represent a cross section from the arc of the show's content from 1964 to 2008. Although there was enough material for ten or more exhibitions of equal value, the pieces that were eventually selected reveal different layers of the remarkable story of Ebony Fashion Fair in microcosm.

Initially during the selection process, the iconic pieces took center stage. But defining what comprises a fashion icon is multi-layered. One example is the Saint Laurent's dress inspired by Picasso from the fall/winter collection of 1979–80. Made of orange silk moiré taffeta with appliquéd swirls of multicolored satin on the skirt; it is a triumph of design and a fitting homage to one of the greatest painters of the twentieth century. A *Vanity Fair* article from 2009[15] describes how Saint Laurent's modern art collection had been acquired because of revenues from *Opium*, his most successful perfume. Thus the art had fed his creativity, and vice versa. The dress is referred to as part of "a dazzling series of embroidered, beaded, and appliquéd evening dresses, exuberantly paying homage to Picasso, Matisse, and Léger." It is also featured on the cover of the catalogue from his 1983 retrospective at the Metropolitan Museum of Art in New York City. The dress held special meaning to Mrs. Johnson, too. In the Ebony Fashion Fair program, *Color Explosion*,[16] the dress is indicated as designed by "Fashion genius St. Laurent" and later the dress is described as a key piece in the show. In fact, the colorful applique on the skirt may have inspired the show's title, "It has cut outs in an abstract design re-embroidered in the skirt to a "color explosion" in a single item."

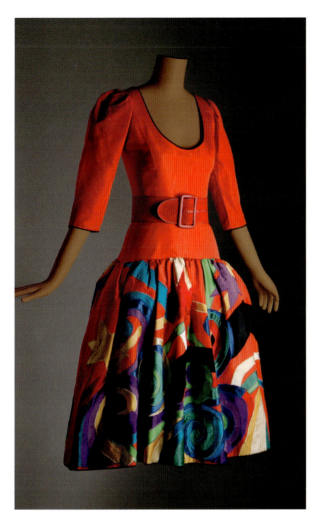

Yves Saint Laurent, 1979
Orange silk moiré taffeta with appliquéd swirls of multi-colored satin on the skirt. The "Picasso" dress was designed as homage to one of the greatest artists of the twentieth century.

Chloe by Karl Lagerfeld, 1983
The "shower dress" is exemplar of exquisite eveningwear that also epitomizes Lagerfeld's sense of humor.

The 1983 Karl Lagerfeld 'showerhead' evening dress for Chloe is a sleeveless floor-length gown made of midnight-blue crepe. The stark front is embellished with only a double vertical row of diamante buttons; the design is reminiscent of crisp menswear. However, like many garments that were chosen for Ebony Fashion Fair over the years, a plain front gives way to a sensational back. In this case the 'big reveal' begins between the shoulder blades, where a beaded 'showerhead' apparently pours a stream of crystal bugle beads down the entire back of the dress to the hem. An amusing piece, it expresses Lagerfeld's quirky sense of humor. In the Ebony Fashion Fair program for 1983–84, the dress is referred to by Mrs. Johnson as his "most outstanding creation" of the season. Mrs. Johnson purchased another corresponding red and black cocktail dress with a faucet on the front, similarly 'pouring' bugle beads down the front of the dress.

Another criterion for selection was evidence of Mrs. Johnson's interest in emerging designers. Two

Emanuel Ungaro, 1987
Yellow and black ruched flamenco dancer skirted evening dress, is iconic for its lavish construction and dramatic silhouette. The dress is quintessentially 1980s.

Emanuel Ungaro, 1971
Ungaro's youthful multi-colored suede patchwork coat and knitwear ensemble radiates the *zeitgeist* of the era.

designers featured frequently both in the show and *Ebony* magazine were André Courrèges and Emanuel Ungaro. Both had worked for Balenciaga whose designs featured in some of the earliest Fashion Fairs. Ungaro's first independent show was in 1965, and he is referenced in the program as one of the designers selected for that year. In the same program[17] Mrs. Johnson proclaims "This year we feel that we have been more discriminating (excuse the term) than ever in our wardrobe selection for the annual EBONY FASHION FAIR. If some of the big name designers failed to come up with new and fresh ideas in their collections, we did not purchase from them. On the other hand when we found

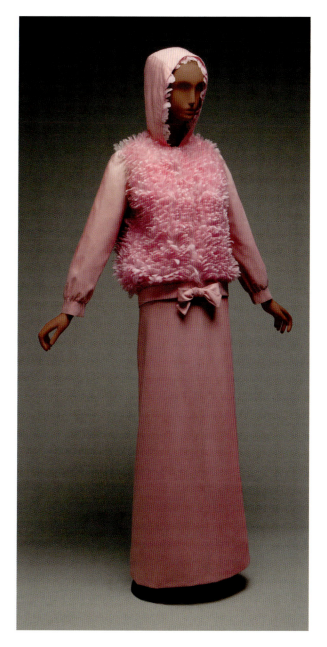

André Courrèges, 1974
The backless gown is covered by a feather-trimmed hoodie. Below, the same gown in its original brown. The plunging back caused a sensation.

a designer with new and exciting designs, we bought like mad." Mrs. Johnson was to continue her admiration of Ungaro's work until he retired in 2005. There are two notable designs by Ungaro in the exhibition; the first is a wonderful patchwork ensemble from 1971. Mrs. Johnson refers to the collection in the Ebony Fashion Fair program *What's Goin' On*. Ungaro is described as "a most realistic and talented designer, highlighted a most colorful collection. With many mixed prints in crochet, knits and suedes, as well as winter voiles, he drew applause from the beginning to the end of his show." The second Ungaro is a dramatic golden-yellow silk satin evening dress featured on the cover of the program for 1987–88, *Fashion Sizzle*. It is symbolic of the "Golden Era" of 30 years of Ebony Fashion Fair.[18] An iconic piece, it captures all the extravagance and drama of 1980s fashion. From the frilled neckline, leg-o-mutton sleeves, and tightly fitted ruched sheath culminating in a black-satin–lined flamenco dancer-style, thigh-revealing skirt that descends to a flounced train at back it's truly magnificent! The style, so new, sensual, and exciting in 1987, became the unwitting model for nearly every prom and bridesmaid dress in America for the next decade.

Back to Courrèges, who was known for his ground breaking futuristic designs in the 1960s. In 1974, Mrs.

47

Johnson purchased a "back-revealing gown"[19] for *The Big Whirl of Fashion* show. It came with a simple, long-sleeved, feather-lined hoodie. The original was made in brown, but the one in the exhibition is pink because Mrs. Johnson ordered it specially made for the show. In the program for the same year, Mrs. Johnson states, "He mentioned the fact that he was one of the first Parisian designers to use black models in his couture showings. "I am inspired, he said, not only by Black models but from the music created by Blacks."[20] Interestingly, André Courrèges, Paco Rabanne, and Pierre Cardin were known as the Futurists for their 1960s design that anticipated a future on space stations. Mrs. Johnson purchased from all of them over the course of their careers.

Christian Lacroix was another designer that Mrs. Johnson followed closely from his early days as design director at Jean Patou; he remained a firm favorite. His fantasy luxury design aesthetic appears to have perfectly coincided with Mrs. Johnsons for the Fashion Fair. His Arles folk-dress inspired ensemble of a black lace frilled blouse with deep white lace cuffs, black and white vertical-striped skirt over a full lace petticoat, topped by red satin fichu-style shawl, was a sensation when it was seen in his first couture collection in 1987. It was featured in several magazines including *Vogue* in October 1987 and photographed on a youthful Cindy Crawford. Lacroix's designs were lavish, theatrical, and feminine. He experimented with lush fabrics in bright colors, textures, and patterns. He often combined the improbable into the impossibly beautiful. The 1980s were a time of extreme opulence in fashion, and Mrs. Johnson, who was at the peak of her curatorial powers, purchased some of the most well-known, photographed and sought after pieces of the era.

Every item in the exhibition radiates luxury. Whether it's the Bob Mackie red and pink custom-made ostrich feather coat, worn over the red and black beaded dress featured on the 1984 *Color Fantasy* Fashion Fair Program. Or the Laura Biagiotti multicolored patchwork mink coat with matching boots over a creamy colored woolen ensemble from the 2006 Fashion Fair, *Stylishly Hot*. Featured in the 40th Fashion Fair show, *The Jazz Age of Fashions*, Alexander McQueen's silver basket-weave raffia gown for Givenchy in 1997 is made from a humble fiber, but the effect is dazzling. The fringed ruff tops a floor-length gown draped on the bias. The bell-shaped sleeves have fringed cuffs; the dress is deceptively simple in construction. The piece is all the more precious because of Mr. McQueen's untimely

Christian Lacroix, 1987
This iconic piece from the designer's first collection was widely photographed and caused a sensation at the time.

Laura Biagiotti, 2006
Fur was a popular material for Fashion Fair selections, and this patchwork coat and matching boots are a fine example of head-to-toe style.

Bob Mackie, 1984
This red and pink ostrich feather coat over a bugle-beaded dress shows the classic Ebony fashion flair for exotic materials and glamour.

demise. Another mark of luxury is exclusivity. The seemingly simple grey wool Dior haute couture coat by Marc Bohan is symbolic of superb pattern cutting. Made in 1964, it is the earliest piece in the exhibition and emphasizes that the fashion of the day was for controlled and refined silhouettes for outerwear as the public face of fashion. Mrs. Johnson purchased from Dior for many years and appreciated Bohan's extensive talent.

Redolent of Lagerfeld's humor, Patrick Kelly's dress "I ♥ Fashion Scandal" was inspired by the show's title, Mrs. Johnson refers to the piece in the program,[21] "He was so in love with our theme this year, 'The Fashion Scandal' that he designed a dress especially for us that you will see tonight that is most innovative." The plain black jersey dress is embellished with Kelly's signature button embellishments in the shape of a pair of eyes over the breasts, and large pair of full red lips over the hips. Kelly, a young black designer with a very promising career, was a casualty of HIV and died of AIDS in 1990.

Not many of the very earliest pieces survive, there were sales of the apparel in the early years, and the funds were given to charity. In addition, some pieces

Givenchy by Alexander McQueen, 1997
Dramatic gown made of raffia, the humble fiber that creates a magnificent fabric and enhances the masterful design and tailoring.

Dior by Marc Bohan, 1963
The simple silhouette of this haute couture gray wool coat belies exquisite cut and workmanship indicative of the spare aesthetics of the era.

did not survive because they simply wore out during the six months of touring with the show, which sometimes ran in as many as 180 venues. More important, because Johnson Publishing Company is not a museum, their agenda was not to preserve every garment that was worn in the Fashion Fair. Instead, the important remainder left after the show was the good work that was made possible through fundraising. Unlike the garments that are out of fashion in a season, the charity lives on.

A FIFTY-YEAR LEGACY

In her lifetime Mrs. Johnson witnessed the widest range of silhouette changes in the history of fashion. When she was born in 1916, skirts had just begun to rise. By the time she was ten, the columnar shaped dresses of the 1920s were worn just below the knee—skirts were shorter than they had ever been. Then the draped and willowy 1930s gave way to the practical, boxy, masculine-styled suits of the war years After World War II, the feminine silhouette returned with a nipped-in waists and ankle-grazing skirts. The 1950s curves gave way to the youthful, space-age inspired miniskirts of the 1960s, reminiscent of the 1920s and the first youth culture fashions of the twentieth century. The svelte 1970s echoed the 1930s and then morphed into the colorful tropical birds that dominated the runways of the 1980s. The 1990s stone-colored columns were accentuated by an emphasis on a fit body. By the turn-of-the-twenty-first century, anything was possible in fashion after the roller-coaster ride of constant change.

It had taken years of hard-earned recognition for Mrs. Johnson to build her well-deserved reputation

Patrick Kelly, 1986
The title of the Fashion Fair was "Fashion Scandal" and Patrick Kelly didn't disappoint with his sensational button-embellished dress.

as a fashion connoisseur. The list of her professional contacts in the fashion industry was awe inspiring. As the fashion editor for *Ebony*, the Fashion Fair director and producer and as a private haute-couture client, her involvement with high fashion spanned five highly productive decades. After the rocky beginning in the 1950s, tarnished with racially related snubs, attitudes had finally changed. During her peak years as the curator of the Fashion Fair from the 1960s through the 1980s, she was held in high esteem and was most likely the most prolific customer for haute couture in the world. During that period, she purchased from the crème de la crème of designers and design houses and curated a fashion brand of her own with Ebony Fashion Fair.

The silhouettes were not the only thing that radically changed in fashion during Mrs. Johnson's lifetime. As the fashion industry grew from the 1950s through the 1970s, it eventually began to founder. By the end of the 1980s, many fashion houses were ailing through over exposed and extended licensing that diluted the power of the brand. During the late 1980s through the next two decades, ailing fashion houses were purchased by corporations that made it their mission to revitalize the brand identity. During that time period, Mrs. Johnson began to lose some of her access to the designers who had been her colleagues and friends for decades. In turn, the designers lost much of their autonomy and became more isolated, surrounded by a corporate labyrinth and guarded by marketing lackeys who had no idea who she was and what she represented. Strangely, it was almost a return to the late 1950s when the Johnsons had begged to buy for the first Ebony Fashion Fairs. By the 1990s branding and use of celebrities in marketing campaigns had rendered high fashion to be little more than a hothouse of experimental blooms; it was as if the soul had been sucked out of haute couture. Success now depends on perfume, make-up. and accessories sales that are scaffolded by the illusion of luxury.

Mrs. Johnson had lived through the heyday of haute couture and the emergence of designer ready-to-wear. Her taste had imprinted generations of African Americans who had attended the thousands of shows over the years. During the half century it existed, Ebony Fashion Fair had toured 180 cities across the United States, Canada, and the Caribbean and raised more than fifty-five million dollars for African American charities.[22] When regarded as just a *portion* of her life's achievements it is a truly remarkable legacy. Mrs. Johnson, who never took no for answer, had turned the capricious perfidy of fashion into a powerful fundraising event. A closing quote from Flügel seems a fitting descriptive of the power of fashion, "The old no longer inspires us with the same sense of veneration as it did; we are inclined to be revolutionary and iconoclastic, and look forward ever hopefully (though our hope is not always reasonable) towards the new. In so far as there is truth in this view, our changing fashions may indeed be looked upon as symbolic of our changing outlook upon many things."[23] Ebony Fashion Fair represented and propelled so much more than fashion alone; it harnessed the power of fashion as a super-fuelled allegory for social change. With that in mind, fashion doesn't seem so bad after all.

NOTES

1. Flügel, J. C. *The Psychology of Clothes*. (The Hogarth Press and the Institute of Psycho-Analysis, 1950), 140.
2. Datamonitor, *Global Apparel, Accessories & Luxury Goods*. (Marketline, 2012), 2.
3. White, Nicola. *Reconstructing Italian Fashion*. (New York: Berg Publishers, 1995), 5.
4. Collins, Jane L. *Threads: Gender, Labor, and Power in the Global Apparel Industry*. (Chicago: University of Chicago Press, 2003).
5. Flügel, 138.
6. Johnson, John H., with Lerone Bennet, Jr. *Succeeding Against the Odds: The Autobiography of a Great American Businessman*. (New York: Amistad, 1992), 252.
7. Ebony 50 Year Anniversary DVD, 2008.
8. Audrey Smalz, interviewed by Joy Bivins, August 21, 2012.
9. *Ebony*. Backstage. September 1978.
10. Ebony Fashion Fair program. 1964.
11. Ebony Fashion Fair program. 1967.
12. *Ebony*. Fashion Fair. December 1959, 177
13. Johnson, 251
14. Ebony Fashion Fair program, 1991, 18–19.
15. Collins, Amy Fine. "The Things Yves Loved," http://www.vanityfair.com/magazine/2009/01/ysl_auction200901
16. Ebony Fashion Fair program, 1979–80, no page number.
17. Ebony Fashion Fair program, 1965, no page number.
18. Ebony Fashion Fair program, 1987–88, 4.
19. Ebony Fashion Fair program, The Big Whirl of Fashion, no page number.
20. Ibid.
21. Ebony Fashion Fair program, Fashion Scandal, 4.
22. Johnson Publishing Company webpage, accessed September 1, 2012, http://www.johnsonpublishing.com/page.php?id=13.
23. Flügel, 143.

INSPIRING BEAUTY

50 Years of Ebony Fashion Fair

SELECTIONS FROM THE EXHIBITION

INNOVATIVE

Tilmann Grawe (France)
Cocktail dress
Haute couture, fall/winter 2003–04
Silk chiné taffeta, horn, plastic and glass beads, horsehair tubing, plastic boning
Appeared in *Living It Up*, 2004–05

Stephen Burrows (United States)
Evening dress
Ready-to-wear, spring/summer 2007
Rayon jersey
Appeared in *Glam Odyssey*, 2008

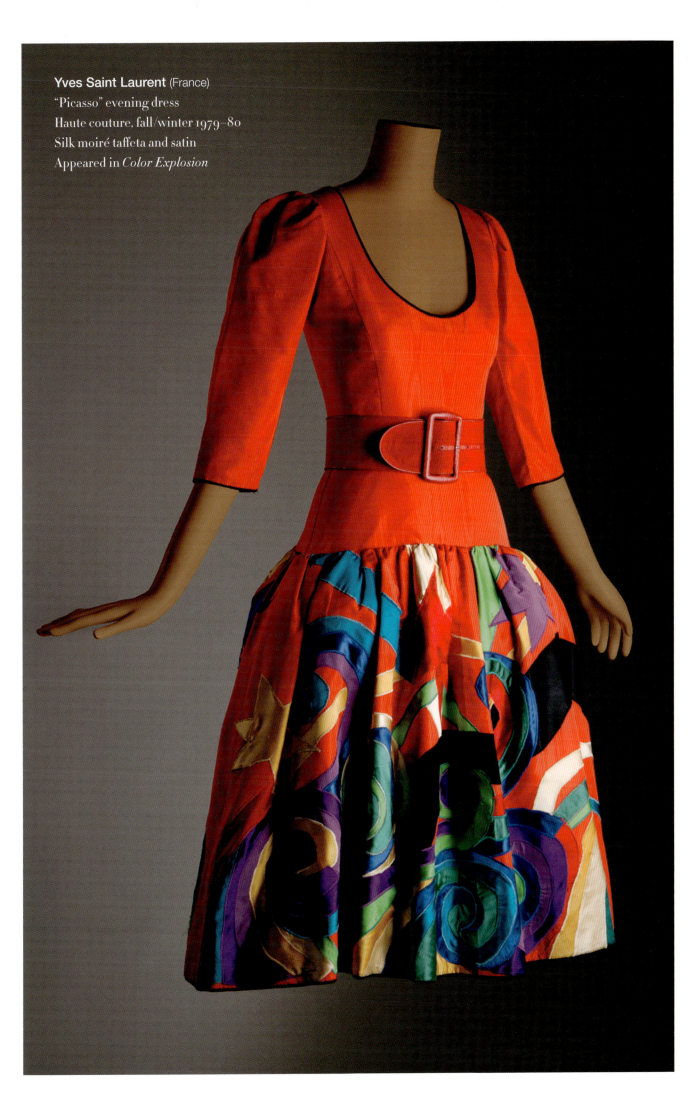

Yves Saint Laurent (France)
"Picasso" evening dress
Haute couture, fall/winter 1979–80
Silk moiré taffeta and satin
Appeared in *Color Explosion*

Christian Dior (France)
Day coat
Haute couture, fall/winter 1964–65
Wool twill
Appeared in *Ebony Fashion Fair with a Spanish Flair*

Pauline Trigère (United States)
Day ensemble
Ready-to-wear, c. spring/summer 1972
Linen

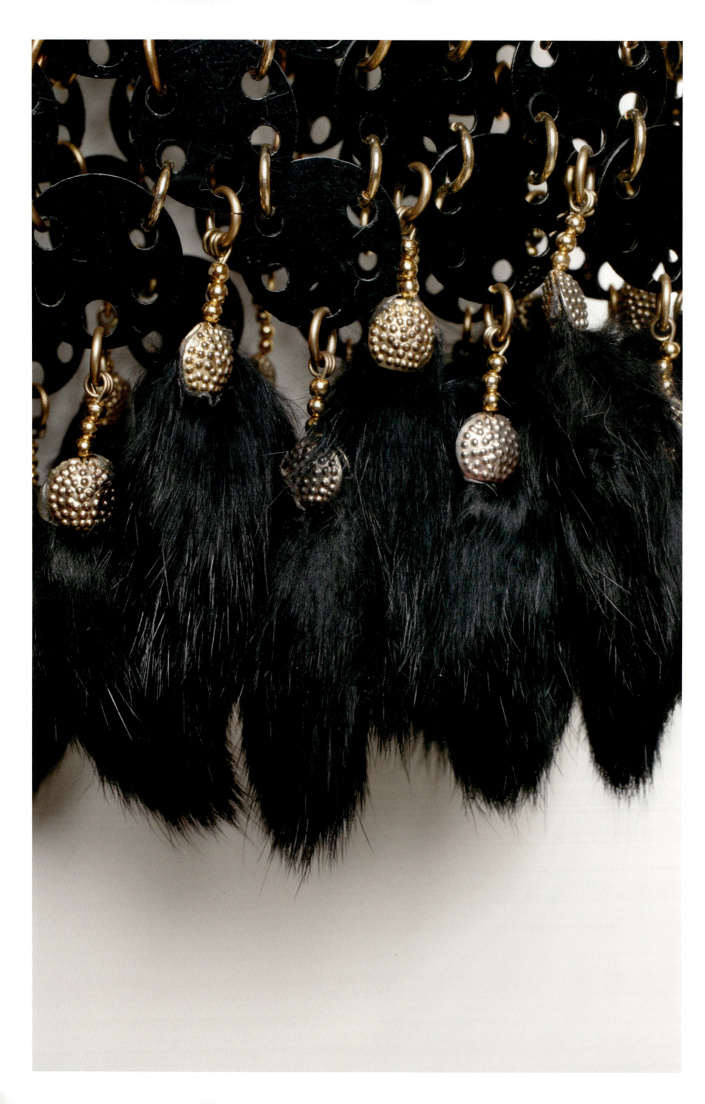

Paco Rabanne (France)
Cocktail ensemble
Haute couture, fall/winter 1993–94
PVC, metal, rabbit
Appeared in *The Rapture of Fashion*

André Courrèges (France)
Evening ensemble
Haute couture, fall/winter 1974–75
Wool broadcloth, feathers
Appeared in *The Big Whirl of Fashion*

Valentino (Italy)
Evening ensemble
Alta moda, fall/winter 1974–75
Silk chiffon, ostrich feathers
Appeared in *The Big Whirl of Fashion*

Christian Lacroix (France)
Cocktail ensemble
Haute couture, fall/winter 1987–88
Silk satin, cotton Alençon lace, silk satin ribbon (infrastructure: synthetic horsehair)
Appeared in *Fashion Sizzle*

Pierre Cardin (France)
Day ensemble
Haute couture, c. fall/winter 1970
Double-faced wool jersey and PVC
Appeared in *The Liberated Look*

GLAMOROUS

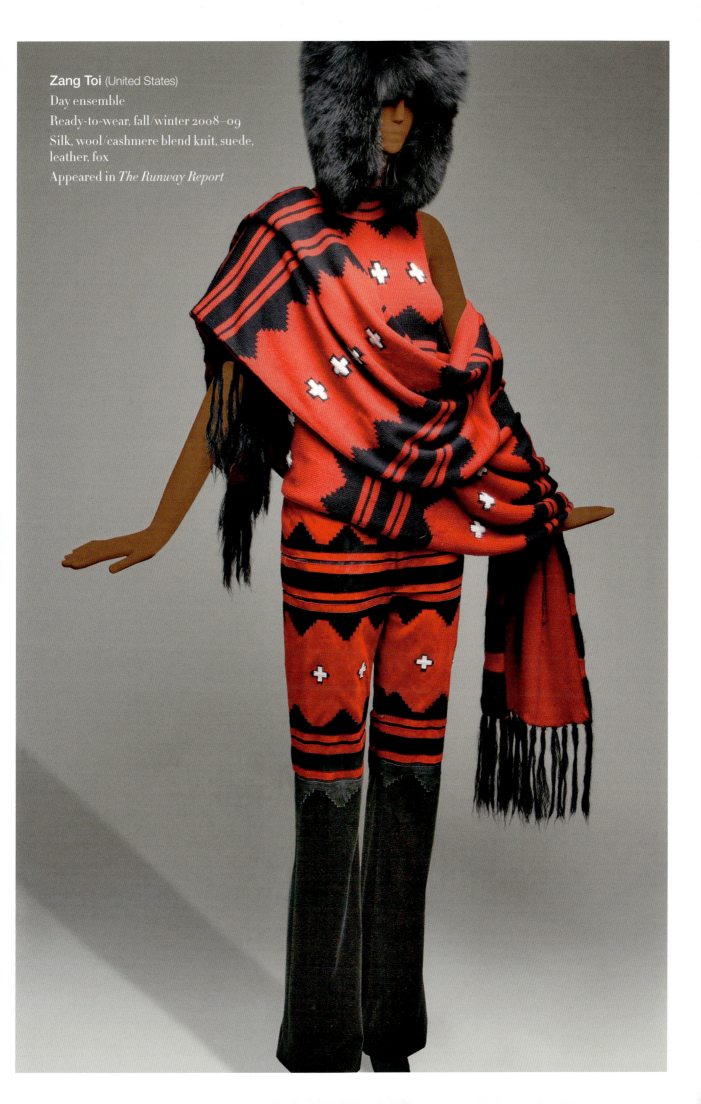

Zang Toi (United States)
Day ensemble
Ready-to-wear, fall/winter 2008–09
Silk, wool/cashmere blend knit, suede, leather, fox
Appeared in *The Runway Report*

Bill Blass (United States)
Day ensemble
Ready-to-wear, fall/winter 1997–98
Wool blend tweed, fox, muskrat
Appeared in *The Great Fashion Mix*

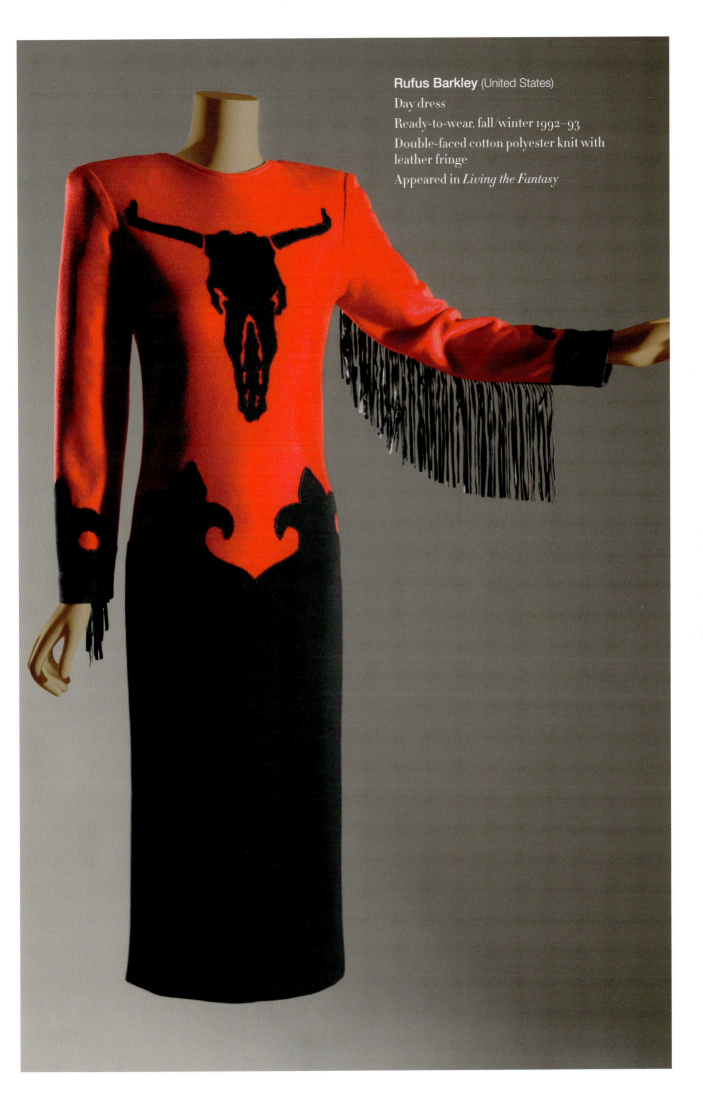

Rufus Barkley (United States)
Day dress
Ready-to-wear, fall/winter 1992–93
Double-faced cotton polyester knit with leather fringe
Appeared in *Living the Fantasy*

Oscar de la Renta (United States)
Evening ensemble
Ready-to-wear, fall/winter 2002–03
Cashmere, silk velvet, fox, horn, cotton embroidery thread, ceramic and glass beads, plastic sequins
Appeared in *Simply Spectacular*

Jean-Louis Scherrer (France)
Day ensemble
Haute couture, fall/winter 2000–01
Fox, goat, mink, Persian lamb, leather
Appeared in *Fashion Sensation*

Thierry Mugler (France)
Day ensemble
Ready-to-wear, fall/winter 2002–03
Felted wool, angora blend, dyed goat, plastic sequins
Appeared in *Simply Spectacular*

Jean Patou (France)
Day ensemble
Haute couture, fall/winter 1986–8
Silk satin, synthetic tulle, silk velvet, feathers
Appeared in *Fashion Scandal*

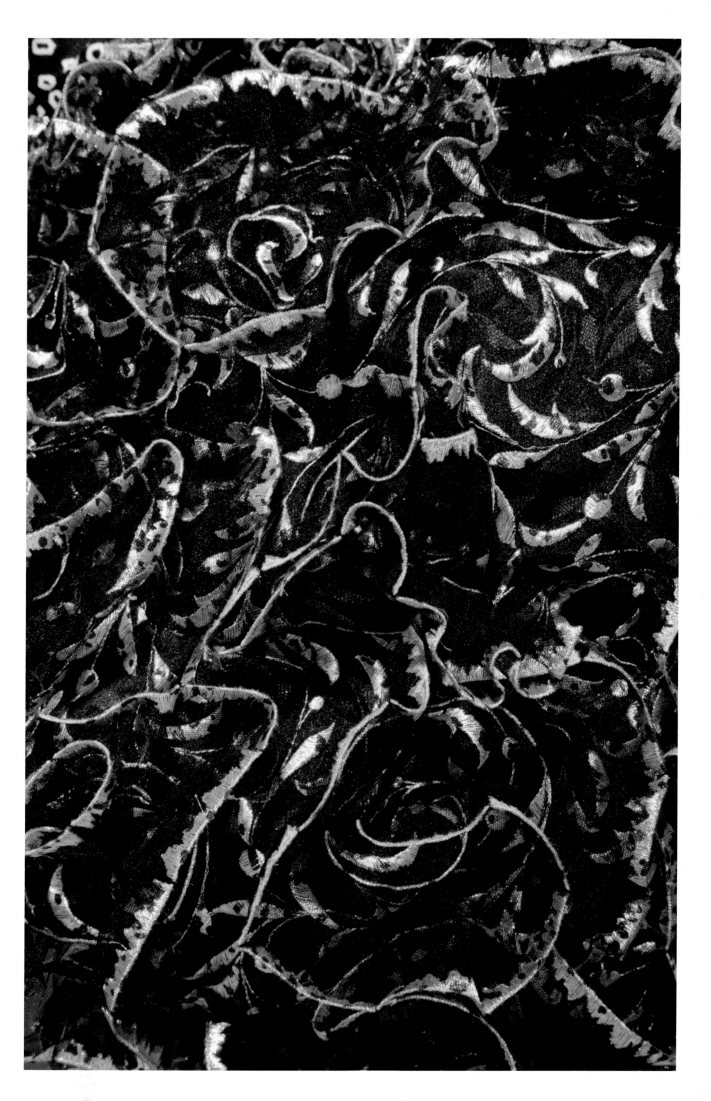

Laura Biagiotti (Italy)
Day ensemble
Ready-to-wear, fall/winter 2006–07
Mink, felted wool, wool gabardine
Appeared in *Stylishly Hot*

Missoni (Italy)
Men's day ensemble
Ready-to-wear, fall/winter 2006–07
Wool/nylon blend chevron knit
Appeared in *Stylishly Hot*

Ralph Rucci (United States)
Day ensemble
Ready-to-wear, fall/winter 2006–07
Cashmere/wool blend, sable
Appeared in *Stylishly Hot*

Erreuno (Italy)
Day ensemble
Ready-to-wear, fall/winter 2002–03
Felted wool blend, leather
Appeared in *Simply Spectacular*

Christian Dior (France)
Day ensemble
Ready-to-wear, fall/winter 1998–99
Wool/cashmere/synthetic blend, metallic thread, fox
Appeared in *Fashions to Love*

COLORFUL

B. Michael (United States)
Evening dress
Custom design, spring/summer 2007
Silk faille
Appeared in *Journey into Bliss and Beyond*, 2007–08

Sarli (Italy)
Cocktail ensemble
Alta moda, fall/winter 1999–2000
Silk chiffon and glass beads
Appeared in *Fashion 2000*

Nina Ricci (France)
Cocktail ensemble
Coat, haute couture, fall/winter 1987–88
Jumpsuit, haute couture, fall/winter 1990–91
Wool, mohair, silk jersey
Coat appeared in *Fashion Sizzle*
Jumpsuit appeared in *Freedom Explosion*

Balestra (Italy)
Evening ensemble
Alta moda, spring/summer 2006
Silk velvet, silk crepe-back satin, glass beads and rhinestones, plastic sequins
Appeared in *Stylishly Hot*, 2006–07

Bob Mackie (United States)
Evening ensemble
Ready-to-wear, fall/winter 1984–85
Silk chiffon, glass beads, ostrich feathers
Appeared in *Color Fantasy*

Todd Oldham (United States)
Evening dress
Special order, fall/winter 1997–98
Silk/rayon blend satin, glass beads, plastic sequins, various synthetic trim
Appeared in *Jazz Age of Fashions*

Coat by Dimitrios, suit by Giorgio Cosani (United States)
Men's coat and suit
Ready-to-wear, c. fall/winter 1981–82
Fox, wool broadcloth
Appeared in *The Look of Elegance*

Emanuel Ungaro (France)
Day ensemble
Haute couture, fall/winter 1971–72
Wool/synthetic blend crochet and knit, suede
Appeared in *What's Going On*

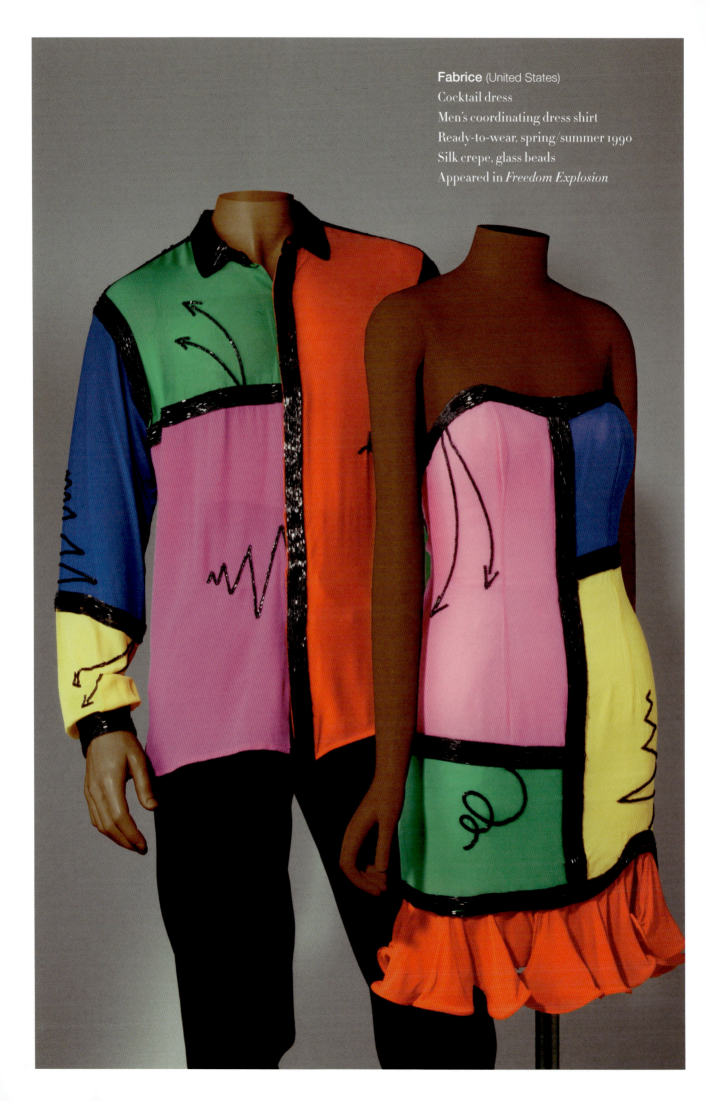

Fabrice (United States)
Cocktail dress
Men's coordinating dress shirt
Ready-to-wear, spring/summer 1990
Silk crepe, glass beads
Appeared in *Freedom Explosion*

L'Amour (United States)
Evening ensemble
Special order, 2001
Leather
Appeared in *Changing Trends of Fashion*

REVEALING

Azzedine Alaïa (France)
Evening dress
Ready-to-wear, spring/summer 1986
Acetate knit
Appeared in *Fashion Scandal*

Louis Féraud (France)
Evening ensemble
Haute couture, fall/winter 1998–99
Silk chiffon, iridescent plastic, glass cabochons and beads, plastic sequins
Appeared in *Fashions to Love*

Jean Patou (France)
Evening dress
Haute couture, fall/winter 1986–87
Flocked silk satin, mink
Appeared in *Fashion Scandal*

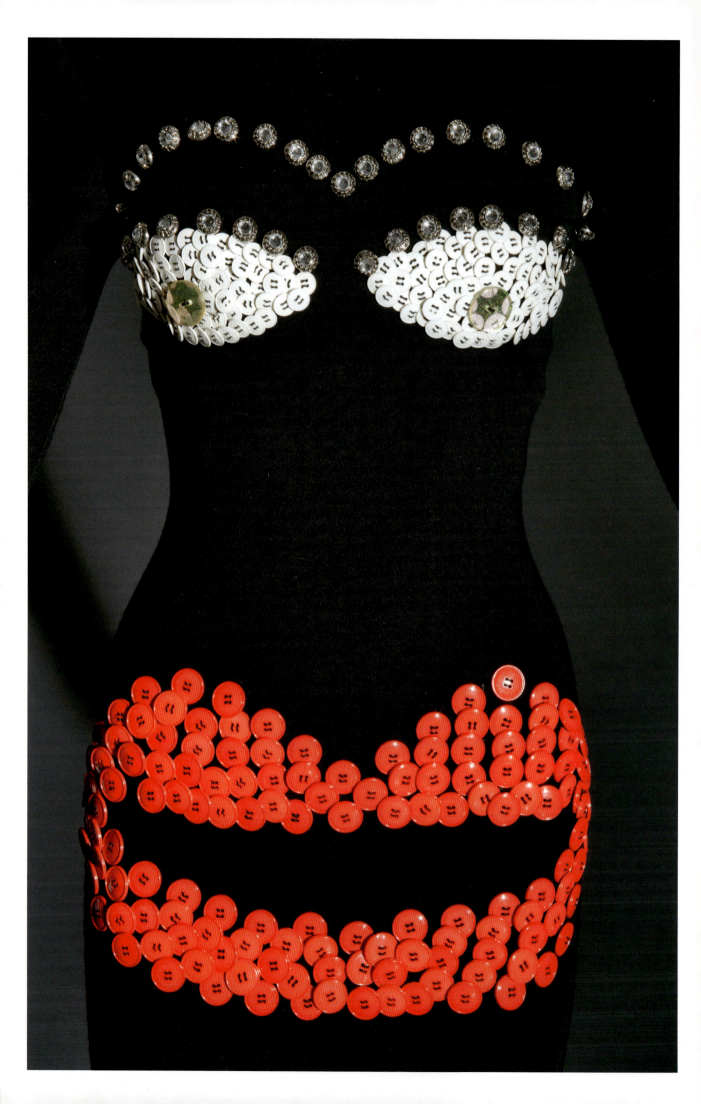

Patrick Kelly (France)
"I Love Fashion Scandal" evening dress
Special order, fall/winter 1986
Wool knit, plastic buttons
Appeared in *Fashion Scandal*

Naeem Khan (United States)
Evening dress
Ready-to-wear, fall/winter 2008–09
Cotton synthetic blend lace, glass beads
Appeared in *The Runway Report*

Sarli (Italy)
Evening dress
Alta moda, spring/summer 2008
Cotton synthetic blend lace, glass beads
Appeared in *The Runway Report*

BOLD

Pierre Cardin (France)
Evening dress
Haute couture, fall/winter 1988–89
Synthetic knit, plastic sequins
Appeared in *Fashion Seduction*

Pierre Balmain (France)
Cocktail ensemble
Haute couture, fall/winter 1988–89
Silk chiffon
Appeared in *Fashion Seduction*

Emanuel Ungaro (France)
Evening dress
Haute couture, fall/winter 1987–88
Silk satin and taffeta
Appeared in *Fashion Sizzle*

Krizia (Italy)
Jumpsuit
Haute couture, fall/winter 1981–82
Silk taffeta and satin
Appeared in *The Look of Elegance*

Issey Miyake (Japan)
Cocktail ensemble
Ready-to-wear, fall/winter 2007–08
Polyester
Appeared in *Glam Odyssey*

SASSY

Angelo Marani (Italy)
Day ensemble
Ready-to-wear, fall/winter 2005–06
Fox, rabbit, mink, synthetic lace and ribbon, leather, nylon/viscose/cotton blend denim
Appeared in *Stylishly Hot*, 2006–07

Ted Lapidus (France)
Coordinating cocktail dresses
Haute couture, fall/winter 2000–01
Hand-painted silk faille, glass beads, plastic sequins, leather, cotton embroidery thread
Appeared in *Fashion Sensation*

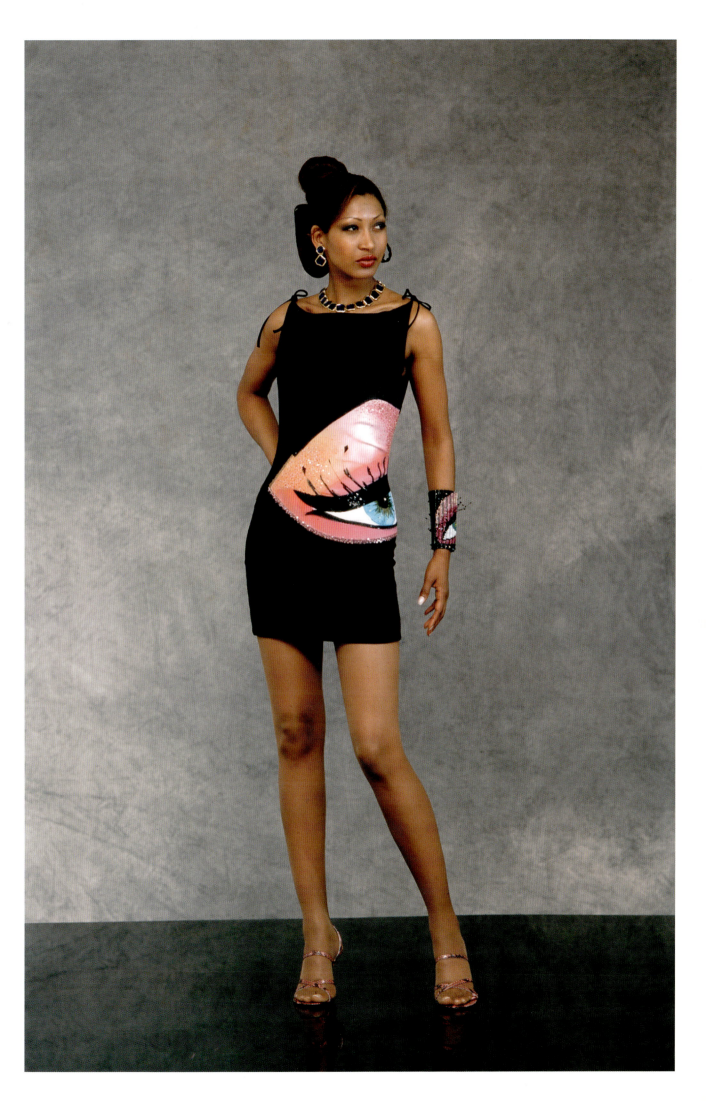

Balizza (Turkey)
Casual evening ensemble
Ready-to-wear, fall/winter 2006–07
Cotton/rayon blend denim, leather, metal studs, plastic sequins
Appeared in *Glam Odyssey*

Emilio Pucci (Italy)
Day ensemble
Ready-to-wear, spring/summer 1988
Cotton velveteen, nylon/spandex knit
Appeared in *Fashion Sensation*

DAZZLING

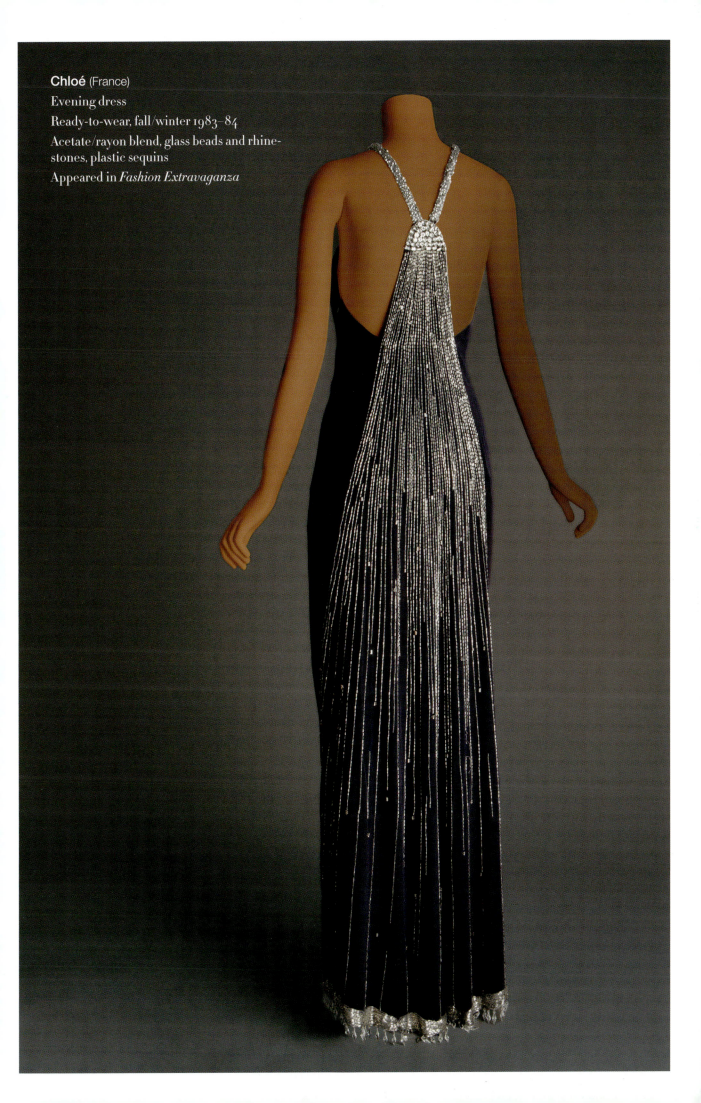

Chloé (France)
Evening dress
Ready-to-wear, fall/winter 1983–84
Acetate/rayon blend, glass beads and rhinestones, plastic sequins
Appeared in *Fashion Extravaganza*

Bob Mackie (United States)
Evening ensemble
Special order, fall 2001–02
Synthetic net, glass beads, ostrich feathers
Appeared in *The Changing Trends of Fashion*

Valentino (Italy)
Cocktail ensemble
Alta moda, fall/winter 1978–79
Silk satin, glass beads, plastic sequins
Appeared in *Back to Glamour*

Bill Blass (United States)

Evening ensemble

Full-figure special order, fall/winter 2008–09

Silk chiffon, synthetic net, glass beads and rhinestones, plastic sequins, ostrich feathers, coque feathers

Appeared in *The Runway Report*

Halston (United States)
Cocktail ensemble
Ready-to-wear, c. 1981
Silk chiffon, plastic sequins, glass beads
Appeared in *The Free Spirit*

Guy Laroche (France)
Men's evening suit
Haute couture, fall/winter 1972–73
Silk/synthetic blend taffeta, plastic sequins
Appeared in *The Mood of Luxury*

Christian Dior (France)
Evening ensemble
Haute couture, fall/winter 1968–69
Wool, plastic sequins, glass and plastic beads, metallic thread
Appeared in *Fashion Freedom '68*

Eric Gaskins (United States)

Cocktail ensemble

Ready-to-wear resort, 2004

Coyote, plastic sequins mounted on silk chiffon

Appeared in *Living It Up*

POWERFUL

Jean-Louis Scherrer (France)
Cocktail ensemble
Haute couture, fall/winter 1989–90
Silk and metallic thread jacquard, glass beads and rhinestones, metallic fringe, plastic sequins
Appeared in *Fashion Magic*

Carolina Herrera (United States)
Evening ensemble
Ready–to-wear, c. 1984
Silk satin, plastic sequins
Appeared in *Color Fantasy*

Vivienne Westwood (United Kingdom)
Ball gown
Special order, fall/winter 2002–03
Silk ribbon taffeta with hand-silkscreened print
Appeared in *Simply Spectacular*

Louis Féraud (France)
Evening dress
Haute couture, fall/winter 1997–98
Silk taffeta, hand-painted synthetic knit
Appeared in *Jazz Age of Fashion*

Yves Saint Laurent (France)
Cocktail ensemble
Haute couture, fall/winter 1977–78
Silk chiffon, glass beads, wool gabardine, fox, mink
Appeared in *Body Attitude*

Henry Jackson (United States)
Ball gown
Special order, 2005
West African woven cotton, synthetic tulle
Appeared in *Stylishly Hot*, 2006–07

Naeem Khan (United States)
Cocktail ensemble
Ready-to-wear, fall/winter 2008–09
Silk twill, silk thread, fox, silk faille, faceted glass beads, silk satin organza
Appeared in *The Runway Report*

Hanae Mori (Japan)
Evening ensemble
Haute couture, fall/winter 2001–02
Corded silk Uchikake, hand-painted with surihaku gold-leaf, silk satin, metallic lace, chinchilla
Appeared in *Changing Trends of Fashion*

Emanuel Ungaro (France)
Bridal gown
Haute couture, fall/winter 1996–97
Cotton/synthetic blend lace, embroidered silk, plastic 'pearl' beads and sequins, glass beads
Appeared in *The Great Fashion Mix*

Givenchy (France)
Evening dress
Haute couture, fall/winter 1997–98
Synthetic raffia mounted on silk gauze
Appeared in *Jazz Age of Fashions*